ENCYCLOP

One hundred copies of this book have been
specially bound and numbered.

A T L A S   A R K H I V E   T H R E E

ENCYCLOPÆDIA ACEPHALICA

Comprising the

CRITICAL DICTIONARY & RELATED TEXTS

edited by

GEORGES BATAILLE

and the

ENCYCLOPÆDIA DA COSTA

edited by

ROBERT LEBEL & ISABELLE WALDBERG

Assembled & Introduced by Alastair Brotchie
Biographies by Dominique Lecoq
Translated by Iain White
Additional translations by Dominic Faccini, Annette Michelson, John Harman, Alexis Lykiard etc.

ATLAS PRESS, LONDON

D O C U M E N T S   O F   T H E   A V A N T - G A R D E

ATLAS ARKHIVE.
DOCUMENTS OF THE
AVANT-GARDE.
NUMBER 3: GEORGES
BATAILLE & ACÉPHALE.

Series Editors:
Alastair Brotchie,
Malcolm Green, Antony
Melville, Terry Hale,
Chris Allen.

Published by Atlas Press.
BCM Atlas Press, London
WC1N 3XX. © 1995, Atlas
Press. © of translations
remains with translators.
Printed in the UK by The
Bath Press. A CIP record
for this book is available
from The British Library.
ISBN 0 947757 87 2.
Published with the help of
the French Ministry of For-
eign affairs, *Sous-Direction de
la Politique du Livre* and The
Arts Council of England.

Permission for French texts:
Works by Georges Bataille
from *Oeuvres complètes, tome 1*
© 1970, Editions Gallimard;
Jean Ferry *A bord du
Valdivia* © 1953, Editions
Gallimard. For other per-
missions: see acknowledgements opposite.

THE ATLAS ARKHIVE SERIES. — The Arkhive series exists to examine and publish previously unavail-able material relating to issues, or neglected groups, within the avant-garde "anti-tradition" of the last 100 years. Where possible they take a documentary format, being either anthologies based on col-lections assembled by the groups themselves, or co-edited with the participation of members.

The first two issues, on *Dada Berlin* and *French Symbolist and Decadent Literature of the 1890s* are still available; these, and forthcoming issues, are described at the back of the present volume.

THIS ISSUE. — This issue of the Arkhive series assembles three sets of texts written by a number of writers associated with Georges Bataille, some of whom were members of his Acéphale group, others being members, or ex-members, of the Surrealist groups in Paris and New York. Apart from the presence of Bataille and his concerns, what unites these texts is their form, which derives from that of dictionaries or encyclopædias.

The first series of texts appeared as the *Dictionnaire critique* in 1929 and 1930, and constituted a separate section of the magazine *Documents*, which was primarily edited by Georges Bataille with some assistance from Carl Einstein. We have re-ordered these entries alphabetically here (p. 157 gives their original order of appearance). The second series, *Related Texts,* also comes from *Documents,* and although these texts were published in the main body of the magazine, both their form and content relates them to the shorter articles in the *Critical Dictionary*. The *Da Costa Encyclopédique* was published anonymously in 1947, in the (highly imperfect) alphabetical order given here, and to preserve its logic we have retained the French titles of these articles.

Consequently, references in the introduction to the texts, indicated by bold type, are given in English for the *Critical Dictionary* and *Related Texts,* in French for the *Da Costa*. Since "Acéphale" was both a secret society and a magazine, it is italicised only when the latter is referred to. References in square brackets are to the bibliography on page 164. Notes to the *Introduction* are on page 25, to the texts on page 166.

ACKNOWLEDGEMENTS. — We owe especial thanks to the publisher Jean-Michel Place and to Dominique Lecoq, President of the *Amis de Georges Bataille,* for their help with this project; to Jean-Jacques Lebel and Michel Waldberg for generously allowing us to translate the *Da Costa;* to Geneviève Calame-Griaule for permission to print works by Marcel Griaule; to Jean Jamin and Editions Jean-Michel Place for permission to print works by Michel Leiris; to Michel Fraenkel for permission to print works by Robert Desnos; to Thieri Foulc and Paul Gayot of the *Cymbalum Pataphysicum,* and to Maurice Imbert, for information concerning the origins of the *Da Costa;* likewise to Edouard Jaguer, Simon Watson Taylor and John Lyle for clarifying somewhat its connections with the Surrealist movement; to Roger Conover for help with permissions; to Michael Richardson for reading, and criticising, the introduction; to the French Ministry of Culture and the Arts Council for their con-tinued financial assistance. We have been unable to trace copyright holders for some texts, for which we apologise. Permission to use the translations by Dominic Faccini and Annette Michelson listed on page 157 in appendix II, originally published in *October* 36 © 1986, and *October* 60 © 1992; granted by the MIT Press, Cambridge, Massachusetts. Photographs by Painlevé on pp. 39 & 40 © Les Documents Cinématographiques.

CONTENTS

ERRATA & REVISIONS. — This reprinting of *Encyclopædia Acephalica* allows for the correction of a few errors, misunderstandings and omissions.

The introduction and its notes refer on a number of occasions to Patrick Waldberg's *Acéphalogramme* which was quoted extensively in the preface to the volume of letters between Patrick and Isabelle Waldberg [F5 in the Bibliography]. This has since appeared in its entirety in *Le Magazine littéraire* (no. 331, April 1995); it adds only detail to the account of Acéphale given below.

A number of reviewers bemoaned the absence of texts from the magazine *Acéphale*. This misunderstanding was perhaps caused by the title of the present book. The texts in *Acéphale* are essentially a defence of Nietzsche in the time of the Nazi party, and most can be found in English in *Visions of Excess* [A20]. The intention of the present book was to present two sets of writings that take the form of definitions, the members of Acéphale being simply the link that connects them.

The picture caption to p. 13 is incorrect: the issue illustrated is no. 2: all the covers of *Acéphale* differed textually, Masson's drawing was reproduced on each.

The biographies on pp.158-163 contain one important mistake. Jean Ferry (1906-1974) did not assume his pseudonym until after the war, he deliberately retained his Jewish surname during the Occupation.

Biographical information about Zdenko Reich reached me from two sources, Richard Walter of the magazine *Infosurr* and Steven Harris, one of our readers in Canada. Reich (real name Rajh) was born and died in Yugoslavia (1905-1990), attended the Ecole Normal Supérior in Paris 1926-28 where he studied under Marcel Mauss. After the collapse of the Grand Jeu group he joined the Surrealists, and there is a text by him in the last issue of *SASDLR*. He was also active in the Popular Front until the war when he returned to Yugoslavia, whereupon the Yugoslavian Communist Party sent him on special missions to England. After the war, like several other Yugoslavian Surrealists, he was a member of Tito's government.

SUBSEQUENT TITLES IN THE ARKHIVE SERIES. — The announcements concerning Atlas Press publications (pp. 171-3) are inaccurate in a number of respects.

Oulipo Compendium appeared as Arkhive 6. Arkhive 5 is *A Mammal's Notebook, Collected Writings of Erik Satie*, edited by Ornella Volta. The next Arkhive will be devoted to the writings of the Vienna Actionists (Brus, Nitsch, Mühl, Schwarzkogler).

It now seems unlikely that Atlas can publish the translation of Michel Surya's biography of Bataille (p.173), the Roussel biography is scheduled for 1999.

(1997)

INTRODUCTION

Georges Bataille circa 1933.

PREAMBLE. — In his *Autobiographical Note*, dating from around 1958, Georges Bataille wrote about himself as follows: "from 1914 onwards, he is convinced that his concern in this world is with writing and, in particular, with the formulation of a paradoxical philosophy." This was something of an under-statement: paradox is present at every level of Bataille's thought, not least because he was convinced that thought was incapable, *by its very nature*, of illuminating the essential areas of human existence. Despite such reservations he evolved a philosophy (or rather an anti-philosophy) of great subtlety and complexity, which developed over many years. His basic notions remained remarkably consistent, however, since they evolved from a small number of concepts, prejudices and obsessions that were in evidence early in his career and which lie at the heart of his texts here (among his earliest published works). Apart from the consistency of his ideas, what is also remarkable in Bataille is his consistency of tone; everything he wrote is vehement, impassioned, definitively "unreasonable." These characteristics are also present in many of the texts in this collection that were *not* written by Bataille: an indication of the powerful influence he exerted upon his contemporaries.

Before considering Bataille's basic ideas in relation to the writings here, some historical documen-tation seems desirable, since both these series of texts arose from particular circumstances and events: principally the rise, and then the defeat, of Fascism, and the periods of upheaval that preceded and followed the Second World War and the Nazi occupation of France. This introduction also gives the first account of the inception of the *Da Costa Encyclopédique*. Until now there has been virtually no information about the circumstances surrounding its publication, its editors, authors, or intentions, (and no doubt this survey contains both errors and omissions). I have confined myself in this intro-duction to a description of the background to, and aims of, the texts that follow, and to a fairly brief survey of some of Bataille's ideas as they relate to them; biographies of the various participants can be found on pp.158-163.

DOCUMENTS & THE CRITICAL DICTIONARY. — The magazine *Documents* was founded in 1929 by Bataille and Pierre d'Espezel, both of whom worked in the Cabinet des Médailles at the Bibliothèque Nationale.[1] Its editorial committee consisted of two main factions who formed, almost from the start, a rather uneasy conception about the direction it should take. The first, centred around Bataille, consisted of writers, many of whom were ex-Surrealists or had been associated with the Paris Dada group or with the group based around the magazine *Le Grand Jeu*. The second faction was more academic, a selection of museum curators, professors of psychiatry and art history. Despite the fact that the chief editorial input was Bataille's, this latter faction included the magazine's financial backer, Georges Wildenstein, proprietor of the celebrated *Gazette des Beaux-Arts*. Each issue was something of a compromise.

Luckily a third group was able to mediate between the two sets of protagonists. The appearance of *Documents* coincided with the birth of modern ethnography in France, and the magazine numbered many of its most important figures on its editorial panel. One of the magazine's founders, Georges-Henri Rivière, had taken charge of reorganising the chaotic artefact collections of the Trocadéro museum, and in 1938 founded the most important museum of anthropology in France, the Musée de

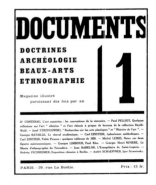

Documents, the first issue, 1929.

l'Homme. He outlined the framework of its methodology in *Documents*,[2] and Michel Leiris, a friend of Bataille's and his collaborator both on *Documents* and in later ventures, was to work in the museum for many years. Another member of the editorial board, Paul Rivet, was the founder with Marcel Mauss and others of the Institut d'Ethnologie, which laid down the ground-rules for field-work which became the basis for all future ethnographic research. Marcel Griaule, a contributor to the *Critical Dictionary*, was to become one of its most celebrated practitioners.[3] Between 1931 and 1933, Griaule led the Dakar-Djibouti expedition, the largest ethnographic expedition undertaken to date, with Leiris as its official secretary.

D'Espezel and his more conservative colleagues were, from the first issue, opposed to the heteroclitic elements which disrupted the articles on ancient and modern art and ethnography to which they imagined the magazine was devoted. An article by Bataille in issue number one — *Le Cheval académique*, which drew typically outrageous conclusions from the deformations of horses on ancient coins — so infuriated d'Espezel that he called for the magazine's suppression. When Carl Einstein suggested a compromise, the creation of a separate section in the magazine specifically to contain these elements, Bataille realised he would be able to use it not only as the platform from which to present his more *outré* ideas, but also to criticise aspects of the main part of the magazine. Thus the *Dictionary*, a magazine within a magazine, came into being from the second issue onwards, its dictionary format no doubt being Bataille's idea, and for a while Wildenstein tolerated and even enjoyed it. Soon, however, essays which would have been more at home there began escaping into the main part of the review (the *Related Texts* printed here), and eventually he withdrew his backing; the magazine folded after two years and 15 issues, its failure to make a profit being an additional factor. In many ways the *Dictionary* is the essence of the whole magazine, its mixture of insight, playfulness, erudition and shock indicate what the magazine as a whole could have been had Bataille not been constrained by his collaborators.

NOT ART BUT EVIDENCE. — The combination of ethnology, aesthetics, philosophy and writing in *Documents* was crucial for Bataille, whose aims were not literary in any ordinary, or even extraordinary, sense of the word. Later he described the magazine as "...an art review offset by an anomalous (*hétéroclite*) section edited by Bataille under the somewhat remote supervision of Carl Einstein."[4] It is obvious here that he saw the function of the *Dictionary* as offsetting the aesthetic preoccupations of an art magazine, and Bataille's one line dismissal of the undertaking rather suggests that in retrospect he may have considered it to have failed, since *Documents* was established to be the exact opposite of an art review, and articles on the arts rarely overshadowed the other contents.

Documents' covers bore the banner: *Doctrines* (or *Variétés*), *Archéologie, Beaux-Arts, Ethnographie,* and from the start it was actively anti-aesthetic. Ethnology gave the lead: it was not concerned with the beautiful, as Griaule stressed in **Gunshot**: "Boring though it be to repeat it, *ethnography* is interested in both *beauty* and *ugliness*, in the European sense of these absurd words. It is however inclined to be suspicious of the beautiful — a rare, and consequently a freakish, event in civilisation." Just as the new ethnography aimed to show all of man, *Documents* took evidence from all aspects of his culture, and made connections appear where they were least expected. It attempted a de-coding of European culture on a par with the emerging disciplines devoted to understanding "primitive" social structures. No distinction was made between high and low culture; only their usefulness to understanding was significant. Many of the writers in *Documents* took this vigorous relativism to extremes on occasion, often in the service of satire and derision, and this certainly heightened editorial tensions between the various factions.

The very name of the magazine implied an examination of the given: not art but *evidence*; not literary writing but *documents*.[5] In this context the importance of the photographs accompanying the texts becomes self-evident, for they provide another layer of information or ironic comment and yet avoid completely the "art" photography later promoted in, say, *Minotaure* (although, according to Leiris, their inclusion was often simply meant to be provocative). Even if, in retrospect, Bataille felt he had not succeeded in making of *Documents* what he wanted, yet, according to Dominique Lecoq[6]: "The failure of *Documents*, indicated as if by well-placed beacons with photographs of the **Big Toe**, was also the success of a way of writing capable of overturning the code of branches of knowledge without, for all that, constituting in itself a closed, complete body of knowledge. Bataille called upon philosophy, ethnology, economics, psychoanalysis, not to borrow their results but to open up the notions they defined in new, illegitimate, unacceptable directions: if logic masks the gaping inadequacies of the logos, Bataille, in impelling *Documents* to expose all the contradictions, chose both to uphold logic and to remove the mask."

THE RELATED TEXTS. — The texts on pp. 85-106 bear an obvious relation to those of the dictionary. They differ from the other essays and contemporary reviews published in *Documents* by the definitional form in which they are cast and this alone seemed to justify their inclusion in this anthology.[7] As I have already noted, this fact did not escape Wildenstein et al., and their inclusion (in particular **Big Toe**, and *especially* its accompanying photographs) in the main part of the review, having escaped the region of the *Critical Dictionary* in which the heterogeneous was supposed to be contained, led to serious editorial arguments and was one of the reasons for the eventual closure of the magazine.[8]

BATAILLE AND THE SURREALISTS. — Many past Surrealists contributed to *Documents*, and they formed the nucleus of an anti-Breton group whose most famous attack on their ex-leader was the manifesto *A Corpse*, which featured a photo of Breton crowned with thorns. Bataille, despite later protestations to the contrary, was the main instigator of this document.[9] The hostility was reciprocal since Breton had attacked them with equal vim in the second Surrealist manifesto. Between the collapse of *Documents* and 1935, however, both Breton and Bataille had followed similarly dispiriting paths in leftist political organisations and their mutual disillusion, and dismay at the rise of Fascism, allowed them to bury their differences with the founding of *Contre-Attaque*, intended as an anti-fascist movement outside of Stalinist influence. Although unsuccessful — it lasted only 18 months — Breton and Bataille remained on good terms, despite disagreements on some issues, from this point onwards.

Bataille now turned his attention away from direct political action to concentrate on two connected projects: Acéphale and the College of Sociology.[10] Acéphale was both an esoteric "secret society" and

Above: *A Corpse*, 1930, photomontage by Boiffard. Below: Leaflet by *Contre-Attaque* for a meeting to celebrate the guillotining of Louis XVI.

a publicly available magazine, and it functioned in the years *between* the appearances of the two sets of texts printed here. Nevertheless, what we know of its aims point to it as the focus for what the texts published here were intended to facilitate.

The College of Sociology constituted the theoretical counterpart of Acéphale. Between 1937 and 1939, its fortnightly lectures were delivered by members or by invited speakers: Bataille, Caillois, Leiris, Kojève, Klossowski, among others, and were attended by many of the leading intellectuals of the time, including Jean Paulhan, Jean-Paul Sartre, Walter Benjamin, Theodor Adorno, Hans Meyer and Claude Lévi-Strauss. Its area of study was contiguous with Bataille's thought in almost all respects, but this is not the place to discuss it and since Denis Hollier's book reprints all the available material in English, the reader is referred to that [A22]. The College examined all areas of social community, an immediate political task being to define possible structures not based on individualism, totalitarianism or the feeble cohesion of democracies. Caillois in particular contributed lectures on the theory of the secret society, which he saw as a sort of sacred ideological virus intended to infect the profane social body.[11] Acéphale was intended to embody these principles in a conspiratorial association.

ACEPHAL. — *a.* and *sb. Obs. rare*; also **asephal** [*a.* Fr. *acéphale*, ad. late L. *acephal-us*: see ACEPHALI.] **A.** *adj.* Having no head or chief; = ACEPHALOUS. (Oxford English Dictionary.)

THE FIGURE OF THE ACEPHAL. — The drawing of the Acephal, a potent expression of the totality of Bataille's thought, embodies his reversed hermeticism in the form of a parody or anti-idealist version of renaissance depictions of the harmonic arrangement of the human body (Leonardo, Fludd etc.).[12] The celebrated aphorism of hermetic philosophy "As above, so below" situated man in a universe designed by God in which the structure of the microcosm reflected that of the macrocosm. Bataille exactly reversed this formula, for him — a heretic exalting the base over the spiritual in a universe in which "man can set aside the thought that it is he or God who keeps the rest of things from being absurd"[13] — the body is projected onto the world: *as below, so above*. The body as trope for society and other structures recurs throughout his writing (e.g. **Architecture**), in particular with regard to the sexual act and orgasm, from which he derived his concept of *expenditure*. To some extent all his writing is a doomed attempt to encompass the tumult of the sexual act (see the final section of this introduction).

The Acephal is headless, not only man escaping his thoughts, but a headless organisation, one abjuring hierarchy (Bataille criticised the Surrealists as hierarchical, and hierarchy is of course the hallmark of fascist organisation). André Masson made the drawing: "I saw him immediately as headless, as becomes him, but what to do with this cumbersome and doubting head? — Irresistibly it finds itself displaced to the sex, which it masks with a 'death's head.' Now, the arms? Automatically one hand (the left!) flourishes a dagger; while the other kneads a blazing heart (a heart that does not belong to the Crucified, but to our master Dionysus). (...) The pectorals starred according to whim. Well, fine so far, but what to make of the stomach? That empty container will be the receptacle for the Labyrinth that elsewhere had become our rallying sign. This drawing, made on the spot, under the eyes of Georges

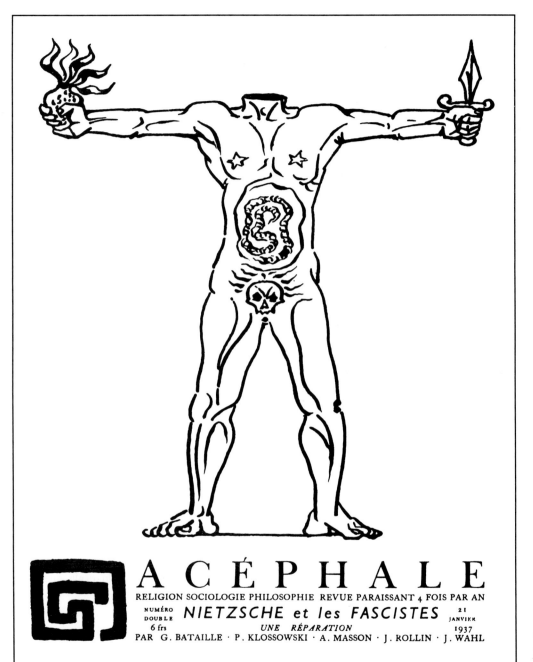

ACÉPHALE

RELIGION SOCIOLOGIE PHILOSOPHIE REVUE PARAISSANT 4 FOIS PAR AN

NUMÉRO DOUBLE 6 frs · NIETZSCHE et les FASCISTES · 21 JANVIER 1937

UNE RÉPARATION

PAR G. BATAILLE · P. KLOSSOWSKI · A. MASSON · J. ROLLIN · J. WAHL

The first issue of *Acéphale*, June 1936, drawing by André Masson.

Bataille, had the good luck to please him. Absolutely."[14]

The drawing inspired Bataille's text *The Sacred Conspiracy*, where he described it in these terms: "Man has escaped from his head just as the condemned man has escaped from his prison, he has found beyond himself not God, who is prohibition against crime, but a being who is unaware of prohibition. Beyond what I am, I meet a being who makes me laugh because he is headless; this fills me with dread because he is made of innocence and crime; he holds a steel weapon in his left hand, flames like those of a Sacred Heart in his right. He is not a man. He is not a God either. He is not me but he is more than me: his stomach is the labyrinth in which he has lost himself, loses me with him, and in which I discover myself as him, in other words as a monster."

THE SECRET SOCIETY OF ACÉPHALE. — Published information about Acéphale is exceptionally scarce, usually ambiguous, and often deliberately inaccurate. Bataille's own few comments appear in his *Autobiographical Note*[15]: "With *Contre-Attaque* dissolved, Bataille immediately decided to form, together with those of his friends who were former members (among them Georges Ambrosino, Pierre Klossowski, Patrick Waldberg), a 'secret society' which, turning its back on politics, would pursue goals that would be solely religious (but anti-Christian, essentially Nietzschean). This society was formed. Its intentions are in part expressed in the journal *Acéphale*, four issues of which appeared between 1936 and 1939. The *Collège de Sociologie*, founded in March 1936,[16] constituted to some extent the exterior aspect of this 'secret society' (...) Of the 'secret society,' it is difficult to speak, but it seems that some of its members at least have retained an impression of a 'voyage out of the world.' Short-lived, of necessity, essentially unviable; in September 1939, all of its members withdrew."

The actual activities and membership of Acéphale are still shrouded in mystery since no member of the group has ever published an account of his involvement.[17] We know something of its aims from other sources, for example, Bataille's invitation to Patrick Waldberg "announced the constitution of a secret society involving a ceremony of initiation, rites, and the acceptance of a changed way of life destined to separate adepts, although nothing would be externally visible, from a world that would henceforth be considered as profane."[18]

Two texts by Bataille give some clues as to his intentions. *The Sacred Conspiracy,* which prefaced the first issue of *Acéphale*, contained an appeal *to go beyond the world:* "It is time to abandon the world of the civilised and its light. It is too late to be reasonable and educated, which has led to a life without appeal." Furthermore: "A world that cannot be loved to the point of death, in the same way that a man loves a woman, represents only self-interest and the obligation to work. If it is compared to worlds gone by, it is hideous, and appears as the most failed of all." Acéphale is, he states, "*ferociously religious,*" yet this religion is atheological: "The *acephalic man* mythologically expresses sovereignty committed to destruction and the death of God, and in this the identification with the headless man merges and melds with the identification with the superhuman, which is entirely 'the death of God.' " (**Absolute,** *Enthousiasme*). God is the enemy of community, or a creator of false community, associated with tranquillity, absence of movement, the finished, time made finite: a prison.[19] (***Eglise***).

The second text constitutes the 11 point programme given to new members. It was not published until 1970, and a few excerpts are sufficient to convey its apocalyptic message. Following the creation of a community, this programme asserts various aims, including the need to "Lift the curse of those feelings of guilt which oppress men, force them into wars they do not want, and consign them to work from whose fruits they never benefit. (...) Realise the universal fulfilment of the individual being within the ironical world of animals through the revelation of an acephalous universe, a universe which exists in a state of play rather than one of obligation. (...) Assume within oneself perversion and crime, not as exclusive values, but as a prelude to their integration into the totality of humanity. (...) Participate in the destruction of the world as it presently exists, with eyes open wide to the world which is yet to be."[20]

The accomplishment of such a programme seems problematic to say the least and nothing is known of what occurred at Acéphale's meetings, although Bataille's written instructions for getting to them allow one to assess their tone: "Do not acknowledge anybody, do not speak to anybody, and take a seat at some distance from other travellers. Get off the train at Saint-Nom, exit the station in the direction of the train and turn left. Follow the instructions of those who will meet you on the road, asking no questions, walk in groups of two or three at the most, without talking, until you reach the path that leaves the road, when you should walk in Indian file, a few metres apart. On nearing the meeting-place, stop and wait to be conducted to it one at a time. Then remain motionless and silent until the end... [the return journey was similarly regimented, and afterwards:] All discussion of the meeting is forbidden, under whatever pretext."

Bataille then describes the meeting site: "On a marshy soil, in the centre of a forest, where turmoil seems to have intervened in the usual order of things, stands a tree struck by lightning. One can recognise in this tree the mute presence of that which has assumed the name of Acéphale, expressed here by these arms without a head. It is a willingness to seek out and to confront a presence that swamps our life of reason which gives to these steps a sense that opposes them to those of others. This ENCOUNTER that is undergone in the forest will be of real value only to the extent to which death makes its presence felt. To go before this presence, is to decide to part the veil with which our own death is shrouded."[21]

Acéphale had other privileged places, including the Place de la Concorde, where Louis XVI was acephalised by the guillotine, but we know nothing of its rites. The most lurid speculations centre on Bataille's interest in performing a human sacrifice. Caillois confirmed this project while recalling his refusal to participate: "The (willing) victim was found, only the executioner was lacking... Bataille asked me to undertake the task perhaps because, while at college, I had written a panegyric to Saint-Just, and so he imagined that I possessed the necessary severity of character."[22]

Patrick Waldberg attended the last meeting: "The war had burst upon us, Acéphale vacillated, undermined by internal dissensions, its conscience shattered perhaps by its obvious incongruity in the face of world-wide disaster. At the last meeting in the heart of the forest, there were only four of us and Bataille solemnly requested whether one of the three others would assent to being put to death, since this sacrifice would be the foundation of a myth, and ensure the survival of the community. This favour was refused him. Some months later the war was unleashed in earnest, sweeping away what hope remained."[23]

Bataille in fact, had been deeply affected by the death of his lover, Laure, in November 1938, and seriously ill with a lung infection, he spent the war absorbed in an internal exploration which resulted in the *Summa Atheologica*.

The group dispersed, some travelling to New York, others to the southern unoccupied zone of France, and yet it possessed an internal cohesion, and with the exception of Caillois (by then living in Argentina), it reformed after the war, albeit in a more exoteric fashion, around the review *Critique* and, it now appears, the *Da Costa*. Other contributors to *Documents* were among the founders of the Resistance; the Musée de l'Homme became one of its principal centres in Paris, the staff forming one of the first organised cells, and the underground magazine *Résistance* was printed in the museum's basement. Early in 1941 the group was betrayed, its female members were sent to concentration camps, and most of the men shot (although Rivet and Rivière escaped this fate).

The exiled Acéphales, ex-members of the College of Sociology and Surrealists met frequently in New York, although their activities were constrained by their situation. Georges Duthuit supervised the publication of a selection of texts relating to the College of Sociology and Acéphale in Eugene Jolas' anthology *Vertical* (1941), and the Surrealists organised a group exhibition *The First Papers of Surrealism*, the first to take myth as its theme, and founded a new review *VVV* (four issues, June 1942 to February 1944).

Meanwhile Patrick Waldberg's work in the Office of War Information had taken him to Algeria, Ireland and London. During his isolation from the New York group he pondered past events and communicated them in a long letter to his wife Isabelle (dated 19 September 1943).[24] An edited version of it, together with responses by Georges Duthuit and Robert Lebel, appeared in the last issue of *VVV* (no. 4, 1944), under the title *Vers un nouveau mythe? Prémonitions et défiances*.

Waldberg expressed a complete disillusion with Acéphale's attempts to create a community based around a new myth, which he concluded could only arise, and not be constructed. The literary and arbitrary nature of its images and rites, its lack of rigour, its Nietzschean bias, precluded its success and yet despite its mistakes he does not quite condemn Bataille, who led him through what he now saw as a pointless labyrinth. Duthuit for his part defended Bataille's appropriation of Nietzsche and Dionysus, but refused to defend Acéphale, not having been a member. Lebel's (another non-member) response was more interesting; he viewed the problem from the perspective of promoting group action, collective activity which, he says, seems to be militated against by some general principle. Acéphale was valid if only because it succeeded in combating this principle for a while, and anyway Bataille had foreseen its failure in his essay *The Sorcerer's Apprentice*.[25] He concludes by proposing that humour, systematically exploited, could provide the cohesion for renewed group action.

Paris was liberated in August 1944, and the foreign exiles began returning, among them Isabelle Waldberg in November '45, Duchamp in May '46, Breton the same month. They returned to a capital in economic and political chaos, in which polemic and accusation reached new heights, even for Paris. Against the background of the *épuration* numerous factions exchanged abuse, formed alliances and fell out again with alarming rapidity. Sartre and the existentialists attacked both Surrealism and the

Communists; the Party replied in kind, refusing to recognise either movement as "engaged" for differing reasons, ideological and pragmatic. Old fellow-travellers attacked Surrealism: Aragon, Tzara, Vailland. The Surrealist group around the review *La Main à plume,* who had remained in Paris during the war, assumed a pro-Moscow position against Breton's group, and suffered rebuffs from all quarters. New movements, such as Isou's Lettrism, arose and attacked everyone, and Maurice Nadeau even published a *History of Surrealism,* by implication consigning it to Trotsky's famous dustbin.[26]

Both the groups originally centred around Bataille and Breton lacked a review in which to publish. The Surrealists' *Minotaure* had folded at the beginning of the war, as had *VVV* in 1944. The next official magazine of the group was *Néon* which did not appear until 1948. An even longer hiatus existed for the Acéphales between the closure of *Acéphale* in 1939 and the founding of *Critique* in 1946. This gap was partially filled by the *Da Costa,* particularly since *Critique* was devoted solely to critical writing.

THE ENCYCLOPÆDIA DA COSTA. — According to the only historical reference available until recently, in the *Encyclopédie des Farces et Attrapes et des Mystifications* [*Encyclopædia of Practical Jokes, Tricks and Hoaxes*],[27] the *Da Costa* appeared unannounced in certain bookshops in St-Germain-des-Prés in the autumn of 1947. Anonymous and deliberately designed so that it appeared to be one fascicle, and not the first, of an encyclopædia being published periodically, it began not only in mid-sentence, but mid-word and bore the heading Fascicle VII, volume II. A few readers wrote to the publisher requesting earlier issues; they were informed that they were all sold, whereas in fact they had never existed. The cover bore a rebus in place of an author's name: *L'âne au nid mât* [Donkey in mast-nest] meaning *Anonymat* [Anonymity]. The author of the article in the *Encyclopédie des Farces,* one "Da Costa," pointed out its "insolence and immoderate use of sarcasm," and the fact that none of the authors had been identified up to the present day (1964). "The next year," he continues, "two further fascicles appeared, entitled *Le Memento universel Da Costa.* The defection of most of the earlier collaborators led to the abandoning of the principle of anonymity, which hardly facilitated the recruitment of new authors. It only remained for the *Da Costa* to scuttle itself, which it proceeded to do all the more promptly since its two successive publishers had pushed the joke to the limit, one having been bankrupted, the second dead. Today, supreme irony, the *Da Costa* has become a bibliophilic rarity, however the time is still not right to reveal details of this enterprise, nor to evoke the very particular violence whose expression it was."

Above: the first *Memento*, 1948, and below, an advertising flyer for it.

This violent expression, so immoderately distributed among the definitions of the *Da Costa* aroused much misdirected anger. The Da Costas, by remaining anonymous (see Appendix I), and enthusiastically stirring so much invective into the ideological pot, were obviously not aiming for reconciliation, and if some of the attacks today are obscure, the result of quarrels long forgotten,[28] those on the institutions of state, Church, learning, etc. are still fresh and steaming (we decided not to edit it). The blackest humour unites these assaults and the Da Costas constituted precisely that group based on a systematic exploitation of humour that Robert Lebel had proposed in 1944.

The extraordinary omission of this publication from all histories of post-war culture in France is not so hard to understand, even given the celebrity of some of its contributors. Their anonymity has been a well-kept secret and was only initially revealed by the recent publication of the letters between Patrick and Isabelle Waldberg written during the war.[29] Since then it has become evident that the *Da Costa* was edited by Isabelle Waldberg and Robert Lebel, with much assistance from Marcel Duchamp,[30] and with Patrick Waldberg acting as a sort of roving emissary (his war work had involved travelling between New York, London, Algeria and later Paris). It included contributions from writers recently returned to Paris, as well as using texts written during the war years in London and New York and presumably collected by Patrick Waldberg. Not only was the Da Costa anonymous, it was hard to obtain. One of its few reviewers noted that it had been "carefully *stifled* by both publisher and the bookshops. Energetic insistence is needed in order to obtain a copy, and the press, with the exception of *Combat*, has observed this conspiracy of silence."[31]

Editorial work on the publication had begun seriously in the autumn of 1946, when Duchamp returned to Paris from a holiday in Switzerland, and by December most of the contributions had been extracted from its disparate authors. A couple of private readings were held in a hotel, arousing vociferous differences of opinion between the Acéphale and Surrealist factions. Eventually these were resolved by voting for each text individually. It was printed by Max-Pol Fouchet, editor of *Fontaine*, who caused innumerable delays. A proof of the first page was made available before Duchamp left for the USA but final proofs did not arrive until March. Further delays arose when Breton reacted with fury to some of the texts by Charles Duits which attacked Surrealism and automatism. Duits agreed to change those texts which most infuriated him (presumably the reference to endives in *Examen* is all that remains of the affront). It finally appeared late in 1947, perhaps early 1948.

Although the authors of the *Da Costa* were careful to preserve their anonymity, Patrick Waldberg noted down some of the authors in a copy belonging to Maurice Saillet, Adrienne Monnier's associate at her celebrated bookshop *La Maison des amis des livres*.[32] Waldberg's annotations are difficult to read and he seems to have been unsure of some of the authors, probably because he was not in Paris when the text was put together. He gives the following attributions, which must remain tentative unless confirmed elsewhere: Ambrosino: **Enthousiasme;** Bataille: **Erotisme, Extase,**[33] Breton: **Enfantin, Esquimau, Etoile;** Brunius: **Ectoplasme;**[34] Chavy: **Erotin;** Chenon: **Euclide;** Duits: **Eloge;**[35] Ferry: **Emeraude, Enclume, Escrocs, Estime,**[36] Lebel: **Education, Engels, Epicier, Estorgissement,**[37] **Exposition;** Waldberg (Isabelle): **Eclat.**

According to Michel Waldberg, however, **Enclume** is by Duits, and his mother was the author of **Encore** as well as drawing the rebus on the cover. Chavy has confirmed that he was also the author of **Egouts**, and Jean-Jacques Lebel that he was the author of **Etc.**, his first publication. The authors of a few of the other texts can be identified. **Eclipse** and **Eternité** are both extracts from Alfred Jarry's *Exploits and Opinions of Doctor Faustroll, Pataphysician* (1911, chapters 24 and 37). The extent of the involvement of Marcel Duchamp as a contributor is hard to assess exactly. Robert Lebel, in his monograph on the artist, confirms that the drawing of the chessboard (**Echecs**) is Duchamp's, and includes it in his *Catalogue raisonné*,[38] which presumably means the chess problem is by Duchamp also. Lebel also implies that the **Licence to Live** (**Emancipation**) was at least inspired by Duchamp,[39] and from Isabelle Waldberg's letters it appears that the overall design of the *Da Costa* was Duchamp's responsibility since he supervised the printing.[40] Her letters also establish the fact that her husband did not himself contribute to the encyclopædia. Some of the other texts are evidently extracts from works included for satirical or ironic reasons (**Edifiant**). I have not been able to identify the source of any of these.

THE LONDON SURREALIST GROUP AND THE *DA COSTA*. — The name of the *Da Costa* had its origin as a private joke among the English Surrealists during the war. Various exiles from Europe frequented the English group at that time, among them the Portuguese artist Antonio Pedro da Costa and the French anarchist Serge Senninger. According to the latter: "One day, one of the Surrealists, Brunius? or Mesens? made his entrance, greeted da Costa and proceeded to greet each of the others in the room with the same surname. Da Costa pointed out he was not far wrong: in Portugal, apart from Salazar, everyone was indeed called Da Costa."[41] A number of the Surrealists and their associates continued to refer to themselves as Da Costas and the habit passed to the Paris and New York groups as members travelled after the end of the war.[42]

Although Waldberg saw members of the English group when he was in London during the war he may not have been actively working on the *Da Costa* at that time. Nevertheless the English group was involved with the project, or one very similar to it, and may actually have initiated it. The group was planning to issue a publication in the form of an encyclopædia in 1945/6 but lack of material, paper, and the difficulties of communicating with colleagues abroad to solicit contributions made this difficult, until it was finally abandoned when its editor, the afore mentioned Antonio Pedro da Costa, returned to Portugal.[43] Instead they envisaged publishing the existing material as a running column in a new series of *The London Bulletin* (which had been the London Surrealist review up to 1940). *The London Bulletin* never reappeared, and one can only presume the English group's texts were absorbed into the Da Costa. Only the entry by Jacques Brunius can be positively identified, and although Isabelle Waldberg urged E.L.T. Mesens to contribute,[44] he may have contented himself with the enigmatic references to the Da Costa that appeared in his London Gallery publications:

MORE DA COSTA NEWS !

Before settling down in Paris to publish his encyclopædia, Da Costa has undertaken a tour of a substantial part of the world. He is visiting Japan, Korea, China, the Philippines and Malaya. In the heart of Navajo land he visited the Mittens who reside in Monument Valley. In the Arizona, he had an important meeting with Max Ernst and Dorothea Tanning at Cottonwood (cables our special correspondent). No scarcity of fuel reported, but short of water. (*London Gallery Express Agency.*)

THE *COLLÈGE DE 'PATAPHYSIQUE* AND THE *DA COSTA*. — The *Collège* is as secretive about its origins as was the *Da Costa*, and until relatively recently, the name of its founder, Emanuel Peillet, was not mentioned in *Collège* publications, nor known beyond its inner circles.[45] The idea of the *Collège* was first proposed during a conversation between Peillet, Maurice Saillet and "Oktav Votka" in *La Maison des amis des livres* in May 1948, almost immediately after the publication of the *Da Costa* and its sequels. The connection between this bookshop and its secretary with the *Da Costa* has already been noted. A

Above: *London Gallery News*, December 1946. Left: a notice from *London Gallery Express*, Mar-Apr 1947. The reference is presumably to Patrick Waldberg who stayed with Ernst in Colorado between February 1945 and January 1947, after which he returned to Paris.

number of other, perhaps tenuous, connections exist: Ferry and Queneau were early and active members of the *Collège*, as were other ex-Surrealists including Senninger, late of the English group. Furthermore, the only text until recently that shed any light upon the *Da Costa* was that of Caradec and Arnaud cited above [F2], both of whom are important members of the *Collège*.

The most persuasive connection, however, is provided by a review of the first issue of the *Collège* review, *Cahier* 1, that appeared in *Paru*[46]: "We must quickly note the publication of these '*Cahiers*' which fill the gap left by the *Da Costa Encyclopædia*. The connection between these two enterprises is obvious, readers of the *Da Costa* will notice the same sort of illustrations, even the repetition of certain images used in the *Da Costa*. Likewise with the texts..." The reviewer, Hugues Montsain, pointed out various similarities. Here it is enough to note that Jean-Hugues Sainmont was one of the pseudonyms employed by Peillet in *Cahier* 1 and afterwards... New facts about the foundation of the Collège are still emerging, and a fuller account should be possible by the time our Arkhive devoted to it appears.

THE PARIS SURREALIST GROUP AND THE *DA COSTA*. — Breton and Duchamp began planning the Sixth International Exhibition of Surrealism soon after their arrival in Paris in June 1946, and it took place a year later. Plans for the exhibition and the *Da Costa* were undertaken at exactly the same time, Breton and Duchamp finishing their outline scheme for the former in December.[47] Its theme was an elaboration of that of the New York exhibition *First Papers of Surrealism* (1942) and the discussion continued by Patrick Waldberg in *VVV* noted above: the search for a new myth. All of the Surrealist contributors to the *Da Costa* also contributed to the catalogue *Le Surréalisme en 1947* (Breton, Brunius, Duchamp, Ferry, Lebel, Waldberg)[48] as did Bataille. Only printing problems prevented the *Da Costa* appearing at the same time; in many respects the authors of the *Da Costa* seem to have constituted an "occult" sub-group within the Surrealist movement of that time.

THE HEAD OF GEORGES BATAILLE. — If the texts in the *Critical Dictionary* (and the *Da Costa*), and the objects and concepts which they define, have a definitively *heterogeneous* character, this is far from being accidental. To appreciate why the apparently random form of the *Dictionary* was so apposite a representation of Bataille's preoccupations, it is necessary to take a more detailed look at some of them. However, this is not the place for a comprehensive survey of Bataille's thought[49] and I have tried to limit this section of the Introduction to that part of it which relates directly to the present book, and to present it as simply as possible, despite the consequent possibility of misrepresentation.

Bataille's ideas are grouped around a set of interrelating notions, many taking the form of more or less unfortunate dualities (profane/sacred, homogeneity/heterogeneity, accumulation/expenditure, thought/eroticism) that are connected principally by the fact that the second portion of each term — which approximates to what he calls "the accursed share" — corresponds to values and necessities that are excluded from the predominant forms of "civilised" culture. However Bataille's ideas do not exactly form a coherent philosophical system (nor for that matter a religious, political or ethical one) in the accepted sense, since he acknowledges as inherent to it both contradictions, and absolute limits beyond which he cannot pass, and when these limits are approached he tends to use images, poetry, even fiction to convey his meaning. Furthermore the texts published here are not straightforward illustrations of one or two of his ideas, but often cover numerous aspects of the totality of his thought, in this respect one might almost look at them as a conflation of philosophical speculation and prose poetry (for example, **Factory Chimney** and **Slaughterhouse**).

Unlike many of his contemporaries, including many of the Surrealists, Bataille considers the moral, ethical and political issues affecting the individual within a social context. From considerations of what it is to be human, he proceeds to social groups, to whole societies. Bataille synthesised his ideas on social structures in his three volume work *The Accursed Share* [A3]; his other large collection, the *Summa Atheologica* [A8, A6 & A14], a more inward-looking work, explores the position of the individual in another three volumes, which although written were never collected together into a single work. It is principally the former, which Bataille himself considered his most important work,[50] and related texts, that are more relevant here. *The Accursed Share* bears the subtitle "An Essay on General Economy" but unlike every other book on economics, it devotes itself to the problem of abundance rather than that of scarcity, and gives as its aim the demonstration that "the sexual act is in time what the tiger is in space." Written between 1945 and 1949, it was prefigured by his essay *The Notion of Expenditure* (1933), itself an expansion of Bataille's somewhat controversial interpretation of Marcel Mauss' essay on *potlatch*, the gift system of North American Indians.[51]

The central thread of *The Accursed Share* is an exploration — beginning in pre-history and moving through various cultures: Aztec, "primitive" and "Indian," and early European to the present day — of the means by which different societies have dealt with excess wealth. These means include sacrifice, festivals and *potlatch* (cf. **Egouts**): transcribed rituals of waste, destruction and euphoric social dissolution. According to Bataille the gradual appearance of capitalism created a profound imbalance in social structures by creating an economy based on scarcity. For the first time the excess wealth produced by the whole of society was hoarded and accumulated so as to benefit that part of it which controlled the productive process: the emerging bourgeoisie. Among the results of this imbalance he numbers war, alienation, slavery and the destruction of community on the social scale, and loss of communication and intimacy on the level of the individual. Industrial society followed the earlier merchant capitalism, systematising and extending the process (**Factory Chimney**).

The world of accumulation is associated in Bataille's system with profanity, homogeneity and stasis. Monetary economy reduces men and all that is essentially human to the status of objects of exchange, to things, to economic slavery, and to the economically useful (**Debacle, Man (1),** *Evaluation*).[52] Yet a world in which the sacred, myth, the heterogeneous and sovereignty are accorded their proper due is one in which relations are not based on the useful, but on expenditure and freedom: a world in which codes of immoderation, sacrifice and excess maintain a social structure which accords value to being rather than utility (*Excès*). Its expression is found in "unproductive expenditure: luxury, mourning, war, cults, the construction of sumptuary monuments, games, spectacles, arts, perverse sexual activity..."[53] This *expenditure* is the portion of the economy that opposes the forces of production and accumulation. In earlier societies the sacred established social cohesion, but in a society based on accumulation it can only represent its subversion.[54]

The forces of accumulation — in our day, of capitalism — are engaged in a struggle to increase their share of the economy, of life. They impose an order based on work alone — in which means become ends in themselves (i.e. work) — which is enforced by the imposition of a strict *homogeneity* upon social relations and activities. The attempt is made to exclude all aspects of the "useless" from existence, activities are valued not for themselves, but for their accumulative worth, conventionally measured by monetary value alone. "According to the judgement of *homogenous* society, each man is worth what he produces; in other words, he stops being an existence *for itself*: he is no more than a function, arranged within measurable limits, of collective production (which makes him an existence *for something other than itself*)."[55] Bataille associates the forces of homogeneity with the Marxist conception of the bourgeois class "whenever the State is shown to be at the service of a threatened homogeneity."[56] The invocation of Marx allows the entrance of the proletariat, stage left, beneath the grimy banners of the heterogeneous. Indeed, the bourgeois consider the worker as no more than filth: "Outside the factory, a labourer is, with regard to a homogeneous person (boss, bureaucrat, etc.), a stranger, a man of another nature, of a non-reduced, non-subjugated nature."[57] Thus the proletariat can perform its traditional Marxian role, and democracy being the platitude inherent to homogeneous society, a means of assimilation and pacification, only the revolutionary function remains open to it. Unfortunately, one might think, the realities of heterogeneous political action turn about a quite desperate ferocity: "Without a profound complicity with natural forces such as violent death, gushing blood, sudden catastrophes and the horrible cries of pain that accompany them, terrifying ruptures of what had seemed to be immutable, the fall into stinking filth of what had been elevated — without a sadistic understanding of an incontestably thundering and torrential nature, there could be no revolutionaries, there could only be a revolting utopian sentimentality."[58] Later Bataille referred to a "politics of the impossible"[59]: because the heterogeneous eschews completion, stasis, the enslaving of the present to the future, a conventional political programme constitutes a servile submission to the possible. Nevertheless, his "refusal to be ruled" allowed common cause with the Surrealists' attacks on the more obvious repressive social institutions of Religion (***Escrocs, Existence, Extasiée***), State (***Emancipation, Etat, Expiation***), Army (***Emulation***), Education and Philosophy (***Education, Evidence, Essence, Explication***), not to mention the niceties of bourgeois existence (***Edifiant, Elégie, Eloge***).

The *heterogeneous,* as its name implies, includes a wide variety of phenomena, processes, and characteristics, united by opposition to homogeneity, or an exclusion from its rule. It does not even fall within the field of investigation, which of necessity is a method whose very purpose is assimilation: "scientific knowledge by definition is only applicable to homogeneous elements. Above all, heterology is opposed to any homogeneous representation of the world, in other words, to any philosophical system."[60] In fact, Bataille's project is impossible in terms of the conventional idea of what philosophy is, and here Bataille underlines an absolute limit to *thought*. However, all is not lost, and a possible way out of this philosophical impasse is offered by Durkheim's definition of the sacred as *that which is not profane*. Bataille proposes a methodology based upon negation: "The specific character of faecal matter or of the spectre, as well as unlimited time or space, can only be the object of a series of negations, such as the absence of any possible common denominator, irrationality, etc. It must be added that there is no way of placing such elements in the immediate objective human domain, in the sense that the pure and simple objectification of their specific character would lead to their incorporation in a homogeneous intellectual system, in other words, to a hypocritical cancellation of excremental character."[61] Homogeneous comprehension only destroys what it wishes to seize, the heterogeneous is unassimilable, it crumbles when exposed to the exhalations of the "frock-coated" professors. And how should one respond to their efforts? By "the excretion of unassimilable elements, which is another way of stating vulgarly that a burst of laughter is the only imaginable and definitively terminal result..."[62] The fly on the orator's nose in **Human Face**.

For these reasons, any attempt at compiling an *Encyclopædia of Heterology* is a farcical contradiction, and the *Critical Dictionary* is not such an attempt, as Bataille makes clear in **Formless**. This text constitutes the core of the *Critical Dictionary*, being a critique of the dictionary itself. A dictionary's sole purpose is the imposition of form and homology, definition fixes objects in thought, extracts them from the world and pins them to a page. A dictionary is never *critical*, any element of subjectivity would allow in the formless, that heterological gob of spittle. **Formless** declassifies and is the negation of definition.[63]

Negation is one approach, but in the introduction to *The Accursed Share* Bataille offers the possibility of defining "a way of thinking whose movement corresponds to the concrete character of the totality that is offered for selection." One can sense his unease with such an apparently tenuous and arbitrary method which, in fact, is either absent from the book or tautological. In many of his other works, including those here, he employs altogether more successful means. An image, a poetic invective, often takes the place of the term in a discourse (like the spider or spit that suddenly end **Formless**), something alien to philosophy, and the photographs in the *Dictionary* perform this same function in a more literal fashion. Finally, Bataille "notoriously" had recourse to that most physically immediate aspect of *literature* — its extreme heterogeneous form in fact — for which he is still best-known in the English-speaking world, namely: pornography (**Erotin**). No wonder then, that Bataille's works must be unclassifiable...

Bataille gave many instances of heterogeneous phenomena; he recognises it as everything *other* or incommensurate, "a force or a shock that presents itself as a charge..."[64] It is characterised by violence, excess, delirium, and he lists "the waste products of the human body and certain analogous matter (trash, vermin, etc.); the parts of the body; persons, words, or acts having a suggestive erotic value; the various unconscious processes such as dreams or neuroses; the numerous elements or social forms that homogenous society is powerless to assimilate: mobs, the warrior, aristocratic and impoverished classes, different types of violent individuals or at least those who refuse rule (madmen, leaders, poets, etc.)"[65] This list can be expanded almost endlessly because actually the power of homogeneity is altogether precarious and its opposition lurks in the most unlikely places (for example, within the scientific method itself, **Explication**, in the basic assumptions of physical reality, **Space**,[66] and of mathematics: **Euclide**, or language: **Eye (1)**,[67] **Metaphor**). In fact many of the texts in the *Critical Dictionary* in particular are devoted to tracing this leaking of the sacred back into the profane, the pollution of homogeneity by heterogeneity, often by considering some topic from the point of view of "primitive" cultures, before pointing out the same features in that of the European (eg **Hygiene, Threshold, Museum, Gunshot**).[68]

The worlds of homogeneity and heterogeneity are simultaneously linked but separated, for example "men who at home are only peaceful and obliging peasants who bounce their children up and down on their knees, in wars are capable of burning, pillaging, killing and torturing."[69] Without the congruence of these worlds no totality of existence is possible: eroticism must coexist with thought, yet homology opposes this coexistence. The sacred, ultimately, manifests itself as "a life of communication, not isolation,"[70] its aim being the recovery of a lost intimacy. Homology desires the opposite, the reduction of man to its tool, and a further aspect of its method is a retreat from the animal origins of man, from nature itself (**Hygiene, Slaughterhouse**). The more "civilised" a society, the "cleaner" it is, history itself being simply a record of the progressive negations of all givens, and the primary given for man is nature. (Even its buildings are a repressive imposition of form on nature: **Architecture**.) Children must be taught a horror of filth and excrement;[71] moral and social status is associated with cleanliness, both metaphorically and actually. The church associates eroticism with impurity and filth, it being the "useless," non-productive aspect of sexuality, just as it denies death and the present moment, or pleasure, with a bizarre but expedient notion: that of an immortal life to come. For Bataille all deferment is a submission to the future, a loss of the absolute freedom in the moment that he defined as sovereignty. "Life *beyond utility* is the domain of sovereignty (...) it is *servile* to consider duration first, to employ the *present time* for the sake of the *future*, which is what we do when we work."[72] (***Economie***). And, at the weekend, why not visit one of those temples of accumulation, a **Museum**, where the heterogeneous is crucified before a crowd whose only ecstasies are the pale effusions of art critics? Meanwhile, exiled to some less salubrious neighbourhood, real rites of sacred horror occur daily, albeit cursed, and shameful: **Slaughterhouse**.

*Photograph (1928), by Paul Citroen, of the Schröder house, designed by Gerrit Rietveld in the purest De Stijl manner, with the exception of a single room.

Civilisation erects barriers between man and what remains of his animal nature (**Metamorphosis**): "The polluted philosophies of Christianity tried hard to separate Life from the activity of the endocrine glands; but they are no worse than the secular philosophies, which separate man from his, let us say, excremental activities. This makes us think of those sublime architects who nonetheless forget that in a kitchen it sometimes happens that water boils..."* The meaning of these taboos, etiquette, hygiene, and repulsions, is simply a fear of death. "What then is the essential meaning of our horror of nature? Not wanting to depend on anything, abandoning the place of our carnal birth, revolting intimately against the fact of dying, generally mistrusting the body, that is, having a deep distrust of what is accidental, natural, perishable — this appears to be for each one of us the sense of the movement that leads us to represent man independently of filth, of the sexual functions and of death."[73] Man cannot escape his body and its constant reminder of his basic condition (**Eye, Mouth, Big Toe, Human Face, etc**.), that condition which separates human from animal: knowledge of death.

Excrement, death and eroticism are thus intimately connected and fenced in by prohibitions which are, however, intended to be transgressed during celebrations of heterology such as festivals and sacrifice. For Bataille sacrifice is the supreme expression of expenditure — which is why it is often associated with the most prodigal expender of energy, the **Sun** — the victim is taken from the real world into a sacred and sovereign realm where death is "the great affirmer, the wonder-struck cry of life" and where what is important is "to pass from a lasting order, in which all consumption is subordinated to the need for duration, to the violence of an unconditional consumption; what is important is to leave a world of real things, whose reality derives from a long term operation and never resides in the moment — a world that creates and preserves (that creates for the benefit of a lasting reality). Sacrifice is the antithesis of production, which is accomplished with a view to the future; it is consumption that is concerned only with the moment. This is the sense in which it is gift and relinquishment, but what is given cannot be an object of preservation for the receiver: the gift of an offering makes it pass precisely into the world of abrupt consumption."[74] In a society in which the sacred has its share, the purpose of sacrifice is "to give destruction its due, to save the rest from a mortal danger of contagion. All those who have to do with sacrifice are in danger, but its limited ritual form regularly has the effect of protecting those who offer it (...) It does not destroy as fire does; only the tie connecting the offering to the world of profitable activity is severed (...) it liberates violence while marking off the domain in which violence reigns absolutely."[75] The alternative: **Man (2), Slaughterhouse**.

As I mentioned earlier, some of the texts in the *Dictionary* so perfectly condense the totality of Bataille's preoccupations that they almost qualify as prose poems. **Factory Chimney** combines a number of his favourite themes: a horror of industrialisation, that machine of accumulation, is here embodied in an impure version of the obelisk (impure because both *functional* and excremental). A factory chimney is nothing but an organ of defecation, the final part of a process of *production* which devours the products of the earth and literally shits them into the sky, blocking out the sun. The obelisk is a symbol of permanence,[76] and the photograph accompanying this text acts as a potent representation of Bataille's vision: the *detumescent* crashing into the mud of the repressive and inhuman order of the *useful*.

—Alastair Brotchie

NOTES

1. Much of this account of *Documents* derives from the excellent article by Dominique Lecoq [C5].

2. *L'Etude des Civilisations matérielles; ethnographie, archéologie, préhistoire* [C1, vol. I, 130-34].

3. His team's work on the Dogon people of West Africa spanned five decades.

4. *Autobiographical Note* [B1, vol. VII, 460]. Not only did Bataille edit this section on his own but he may also have re-written some of the articles in it (Einstein for example did not write French), and it seems likely he also suggested subjects, and their possible treatment, to other contributors.

5. One can only assume that the anti-Bataille faction had not envisaged this examination extending to their *own* milieu.

6. [C5, 125.]

7. Two other essays by Bataille could possibly have been included: *Le Langage des fleurs* (Series I, 3) and *L'Esprit moderne et le jeu des transpositions* (Series II, 8), but they did not seem entirely to embody the spirit of the dictionary.

8. As Leiris has made clear, none of this was accidental [C6]: "In issue 3 (of *Documents*) Bataille gives a first rough outline of the aggressively anti-idealist philosophy he was to embrace... Yet it was not until issue 4 that Bataille — the obstinate peasant, who could appear as though he were not up to anything, yet not let go of his idea — decided to put his cards on the table. Illustrated

with photographs, one of which, taken in 1905, shows a lower-middle-class wedding with impossible embellishments, the others theatre people and other characters dating from the turn of the century at the very latest, but with incredibly antiquated clothing, poses, or physiognomies, **Human Face** is a real outrage that Bataille, in presenting this clownish gallery of creatures with 'madly improbable' appearances, actually men and women who could be our fathers and mothers, is perpetrating against the reassuring idea of a human nature whose continuity would imply 'the permanence of certain conspicuous qualities' and against the very idea of 'inserting nature into the order of reason.' Soon after came **Big Toe**, with which Bataille took a firm stand (so to speak): full-page reproductions of friendly big toes and a commentary setting out to argue that if the foot is laden with taboos and is an object of erotic fetishism, this is because it reminds man, whose feet are planted in the mud and whose head is raised towards heaven, that his life is no more than a 'back and forth movement from ordure to ideal and ideal back to ordure.' " (Translation by Lydia Davis.)

9. He describes its inception in *Un Cadavre* [A2, 30].

10. Or three if one includes Bataille's vice-presidency of the *Société de psychologie collective*. I am grateful to Dominique Lecoq for pointing out a general omission in this introduction, namely the importance of psychoanalysis in Bataille's work and especially in the *Dictionary*, which proceeds in an associative manner deriving from analysis and based upon "the tasks of words" (**Formless**).

11. *Brotherhoods, Orders, Secret Societies, Churches* [A22, 145-158]. The appendices to this book also contain an important letter from Bataille to Caillois about the Acéphale project (356-359).

12. Leiris wrote a study of two such diagrams in *Documents* (I, 48-52).

13. *The Sacred Conspiracy* [A20, 180].

14. From *Le Soc de la charrue* [E5].

15. [B1, vol. VII.]

16. In fact the College dates from a year later.

17. A provisional list of members would include: Georges Bataille, Colette Peignot (Laure), Georges Ambrosino, Pierre Andler (pseud. of Pierre Dugan), Jacques Chavy, René Chenon, George Dussat, Jean Rollin, Pierre or Imre Keleman, Patrick and

Isabelle Waldberg, Roger Caillois, Pierre Klossowski, Jean Dautry, Henri Dubief and perhaps Jules Monneret. Some of these names are obscure. Dominique Lecoq was able to supply some information: Dubief & Dautry were historians, associated with Souvarine's *Cercle Communiste Démocratique* and later *Contre-Attaque;* Dussat, an unpublished poet; and Keleman a Hungarian refugee and professional translator. (See biographies, p. 158).

18. [F5, 8.]

19. *Propositions on the Death of God* [A20, 199 & 201.]

20. *Programme*, dated 4/4/36 [B1, vol. II, 274].

21. [C3.]

22. Cited in J.-P. Le Bouler, *Bataille et Caillois, divergences et complicités* [E9, 47]. According to Tatsuo Satomi, the suicide of the Japanese writer Yukio Mishima was inspired by Bataille's interest in human sacrifice, ibid, p. 55.

23 *Acéphalogramme*, unpublished text quoted in [F5, 9].

24. [F5, 84-89.]

25. Included in [A22, 12-23].

26. The best English account of these debates, although from a year or so later, is to be found in the six issues of *Transition 48* (later *49* and *50*). Sartre, Bataille, and Fouchet were all on its editorial board.

27. [F2.]

28. Such as those on the existentialists led by Sartre: ***Estorgissement, Erratum, Essence, Evangelique***.

29. [F5]. It is not mentioned in the massive catalogue to the *Paris, Paris* (1937-1957) exhibition held at the Centre Georges Pompidou in 1981, nor was it mentioned by *Critique*, despite the fact that many of its reviewers contributed to it; likewise Patrick Waldberg's chronology in his *Surrealism* (Thames & Hudson, 1965), omits any reference.

30. In his *Marcel Duchamp* (Trianon Press, London, 1959, p. 55) Lebel confirms Duchamp's involvement with the *Da Costa* during his stay in Paris between May 1946 and January 1947; his son Jean-Jacques Lebel, who was present at the editorial meetings in their apartment, also recalls Duchamp taking an active and important role. Simon Watson Taylor similarly identified Duchamp as one of its editors both in

Paris and New York (letter to the editor).

31. Hector Niel, *Paru*, February 1948, p. 65. The review notes that this hostility, as well as equal adoration in some quarters, is because the *Da Costa* is both threatening and offensive, and displays a total disrespect for ideas, people and even intelligence (the deliberate stupidity of **Eloge** being cited). The first *Memento* was also reviewed in *Paru* (December 1948, 53-54).

32. My thanks to the present owner of the shop, Maurice Imbert, who owns this copy of the *Da Costa*.

33. However, Jacques Chavy does not believe that Bataille contributed to the Da Costa, despite Isabelle Waldberg's letters which unequivocally state the opposite.

34. **Ectoplasme** later appeared under Brunius' name in the *Humour poétique* issue of *La Nef*, 71/2, Dec 1950/Jan. 1951..

35. Curiously, Patrick Waldberg misspells his name as *Duys,* and if Duits was the author of **Eloge**, one imagines that he must be the author of **Entité**, **Erudition**, **Etendard**, **Euphorie**, **Examen** and **Exempt**. However, Isabelle Waldberg mentions a number of joint texts by Duits and Lebel, perhaps referring to this sequence. (Letter of 30.12.1946.)

36. Ferry's Ms. of **Escrocs** was recently discovered at the Organon of the Collège de 'Pataphysique, and **Estime** later reappeared as *A Bord du "Valdivia"* in Ferry's short story collection *Le Mécanicien* (1950).

37. Waldberg has a question mark after this attribution, and there is some suspicion that this may be the work of Peillet. (See note 45.)

38. Robert Lebel, op. cit., item 192, p. 175. Schwarz, however, (*The Complete Works of Marcel Duchamp*, Thames and Hudson, 1969, 593) is of the opposite opinion, but he was writing later than Robert Lebel, one of the *Da Costa's* editors, and he seems to have confused the various appearances of the *Da Costa*, not realising that *Memento I* is actually the second issue.

39. Op. cit., 34.

40. Letters of 10.1.47 and 7.2.47. Duchamp was an experienced typographer and had designed many books for the Surrealists and others since the 1920s. Given the immense critical opus smothering Duchamp it is surprising that his work as a book designer has so far escaped academic dissection.

41. Letter of 10 May 1990 to Thieri Foulc. Edouard Jaguer tells essentially the same story except that in his version it is Breton meeting Antonio Da Costa and Candido Costa Pinto in a café in Paris (letter to the editor 21/5/92). Senninger's version would be the earlier since Antonio Pedro left London for Portugal late in 1945 and stayed there until travelling to Paris for the Surrealist exhibition in June 47; also Isabelle Waldberg was using the term before Breton's return to Paris in May 1946.

42. "Your return to the Da Costa family pleases me very much, especially as you seem to see this name as a way of nullifying the Parisian tendency to be over serious." Letter from Isabelle to Patrick Waldberg, 18. 2. 1946.

43. Unpublished letter from Brunius to Maurice Henry, 10.1.46.

44. Letter to Patrick Waldberg, 20 Dec. 1946. Mesens had edited *The London Bulletin* and directed the activities of the English Surrealist Group from the London Gallery.

45. Peillet's name was first revealed publicly in the novel by Henri Thomas, *Une Saison volée*, Gallimard, 1986. Thomas' book describes the foundation of the *Collège*, but is wildly inaccurate in many places.

46. July 1950.

47. The English Group, for example, received a complete layout, and invitation to participate, from Breton in January (unpublished letter from Breton to Brunius, 12.1.47).

48. All were also signatories to the manifesto *Rupture inaugurale* which accompanied the exhibition and re-stated Surrealism's ethical, political and artistic positions.

49. For such a survey in English see [E3].

50. According to Métraux [E5, 680].

51. First published in 1925 [H1]. *The Notion of Expenditure* is included in *Visions of Excess* [A20]. Bataille and Mauss both saw economic exchange in moral rather than rational terms, i.e. primarily intended to maintain relationships, but Mauss attributed to *potlatch* an obligatory aspect that Bataille ignored in his interpretation of it.

52. According to Bataille, Marx's project was the reverse, "to reduce things to the condition of man" but in practical terms Communism could not achieve this (*Accursed Share*, I, 135 & 141). Likewise religion, in its Christian guise, simply administers,

polices, and regulates expenditure, rather than satisfying it.

53. *The Notion of Expenditure* [A20, 118].

54. [A2, 107]

55. *The Psychological Structure of Fascism* [A20, 138]. Cf. "Free" market policies of Thatcherism, Reaganism etc.

56. [A20, 139.]

57. [A20, 138.]

58. *The Use Value of D.A.F. de Sade* [A2, 101]. Bataille soon modified this opinion, believing that in practice, Communism was bureaucratic and repressive.

59. For example in [B1, vol. III, 520].

60. [A2, 97.]

61. [A2, 98.]

62. [A2, 99.]

63. It is precisely the exclusive and definitive quality of dictionaries that have made them of interest to various writers and there are a number of obvious precursors of the *Critical Dictionary* which have exploited these qualities by subversion. More or less successful examples include Flaubert's *Dictionary of Received Ideas*, Bierce's *Devil's Dictionary*, Eluard & Breton's *Dictionnaire abrégé du surréalisme*.

Two of the contributors to the *Critical Dictionary* had also written dictionaries of their own. In Leiris' *Glossaire: j'y serre mes gloses* (which first appeared in *La Révolution surréaliste*), new meanings are found *inside* words, suggested by their phonetics, attached to the original, but sufficiently fluid to admit the subjective, and are thus infected with emotion, penetrated by the *formless*. Artaud commented: "Yes, from now on language has only one use — as a means for madness, for the elimination of thought, for rupture, a labyrinth of irrationality, not a DICTIONARY where certain pedants in the neighbourhood of the Seine channel their spiritual strictures."

Einstein's *Encyclopædia Bittanica*, subtitled a *Handbook of Art Knowledge*, put forward less radical definitions:

SCULPTURE. — Take a bit of this and a bit of that, position in space and make assertions. If lacking in courage, enter the Collection of Drainpipes, head held high, and discourse upon historical continuity.

MERDE. — Value judgement of a sensitive idealist anticipating a private paradise.

64. [A2, 143.]

65. [A2, 142.]

66. Where the heterogeneous appears as the image of "an ape dressed as a woman"!

67.. *Argot* being the heterogeneous aspect of language, which the *Académie* attempts to suppress: **Eye (4)**.

68. Likewise Bataille demonstrates the existence of *potlatch* in Europe, as exemplified by *champagne*, which he rather coyly describes as "animated by the movement of general exuberance and clearly symbolic of overflowing energy." [A3, vol. II, 41.]

69. [A3, vol. II, 22.] The traditional Christian messengers between these two domains being **Angels**.

70. Cf. *Sacrifice* [E7, 66].

71. Although Bataille notes "I imagine that our disgust for excrement... is because of something other than its objective reality. But my impression is contrary to the one that generally prevails, and I don't feel obliged to be convincing on this point."! [A3, vol. II, 72.]

72. [A3, vol. II 198.] It did not escape him that writing a book was precisely such an employment.

73. [A3, vol. II, 91] Thus, Bataille continues: "The line of development from taboos on incest or menstrual blood to the religions of purity and of the soul's immortality are clear."

74. [A18, 46 & 49.]

75. [A3, vol. I, 58-9.]

76. "The obelisk is without a doubt the purest image of the head and of the heavens... And even today, wherever its rigid image stands out against the sky, it seems that sovereign permanence is maintained across the unfortunate vicissitudes of civilisations." [A20, 215.]

The actress Bessie Love playing an angel.

of being. I have myself a thousand times seen them in garments different from those in which I had seen them previously...

"The angels live among themselves as men live on earth; they have lodgings and houses, more or less magnificent according to the rank of each. I have sometimes conversed with angels concerning this; they told me they were greatly surprised that those who gave themselves out as being learned, and were reputed as such in the Church and the world were as ignorant as they are concerning this matter, after having heard from Jesus Christ himself that in his Father's house there are many mansions.

"I know from my own experience what I have called angels' dwellings, for every time I have spoken with them, I have done so in their quarters and I have found these similar to the habitations of men on earth: but nevertheless far more beautiful. In them are seen porticoes, courtyards, vestibules, antechambers, bedrooms, living-rooms, halls, flower beds, gardens, orchards and fields." (Emmanuel Swedenborg, *The Marvels of Heaven and Hell*.)

"*Note.* — The reason Milton wrote in fetters when he wrote of Angels & God, and at liberty when of Devils & Hell, is because he was a true Poet and of the Devil's party without knowing it." (William Blake, *The Marriage of Heaven and Hell*.)

Above: The angel Gabriel from a 12th century Spanish miniature (Codex Vigilano). Right: The Negro actor Wesley Hill playing the angel Gabriel in the film *The Green Pastures*.

2. *The Angel Gabriel.* "GABRIEL (from a Hebrew word which strictly means the *man of God*), archangel who came to the Virgin to announce that she was to be the mother of Jesus Christ (Luke, 1. 26ff.).

— Occult sciences and astrology. Genius of the Moon, presiding over the ninth circle of light in the hermetic hierarchy." (*Nouvelle Larousse Illustré*.)

Scripture cites the archangels Gabriel, Michael and Raphaël as chiefs of the heavenly hosts that vanquished Lucifer and the rebel angels.

In the *Sepher Henoch*, ch. XX, we read: "Gabriel, one of the holy angels, who presides over Ikisat, over Paradise and the Cherubim..."

According to the *Sepher Henoch*, ch. LXIX, one of the guilty angels was likewise called Gabriel. "It is he who revealed to the sons of men how to kill; it was he who seduced Eve and taught the sons of men deadly wounds, the breastplate, the buckler, the sword, and all things that can kill or avoid death. He formed the inhabitants of the arid element down to the consummation of the centuries."

With Michaël and Samaël, Gabriel is the angel who presides over Monday. His residence is in the Little Bear.

ARCHITECTURE. — Architecture is the expression of the true nature of societies, as physiognomy is the expression of the nature of individuals. However, this comparison is applicable, above all, to the physiognomy of officials (prelates, magistrates, admirals). In fact, only society's ideal nature — that of authoritative command and prohibition — expresses itself in actual architectural constructions. Thus great monuments rise up like dams, opposing a logic of majesty and authority to all unquiet elements; it is in the form of cathedrals and palaces that Church and State speak to and impose silence upon the crowds. Indeed, monuments obviously inspire good social behaviour and often even genuine fear. The fall of the Bastille is symbolic of this state of things. This mass movement is difficult to explain otherwise than by popular hostility towards monuments which are their veritable masters.

For that matter, whenever we find *architectural construction* elsewhere than in monuments, whether it be in physiognomy, dress, music, or painting, we can infer a prevailing taste for human or divine *authority*. The large-scale compositions of certain painters express the will to constrain the spirit within an official ideal. The disappearance of academic pictorial composition, on the other hand, opens the path to the expression (and thereby the exaltation) of psychological processes distinctly at odds with social stability. This, in large part, explains the strong reaction elicited, for over half a century, by the progressive transformation of painting, hitherto characterised by a sort of concealed architectural skeleton.

It is clear, in any case, that mathematical order imposed upon stone is really the culmination of the evolution of earthly forms, whose direction is indicated within the biological order by the passage from the simian to the human form, the latter already displaying all the elements of architecture. Man would seem to represent merely an intermediary stage within the morphological development between monkey and building. Forms have become increasingly static, increasingly dominant. From the very outset, in any case, the human and architectural orders make common cause, the latter being only the development of the former. Therefore an attack on architecture, whose monumental productions now truly dominate the whole earth, grouping the servile multitudes under their shadow, imposing admiration and wonder, order and constraint, is necessarily, as it were, an attack on man. Currently, an entire earthly activity, and undoubtedly the most intellectually outstanding, tends, through the denunciation of human dominance, in this direction. Hence, however strange this may seem when a creature as elegant as the human being is involved, a path — traced by the painters — opens up toward bestial monstrosity, as if there were no other way of escaping the architectural straitjacket.

BENGA (Féral). — The young Senegalese dancer Féral Benga, who is at present starring in the revue at the Folies-Bergère, was born in Dakar in 1906. He made his debut in 1925 among the extras at the Folies-Bergère, then drew attention to himself in 1926 in a parody of Josephine Baker, whom he interpreted with Dorville, to music by G.H. Rivière.

With all due deference to paleface chauvinism, it is interesting to note that, at least in the domain of show-business, the deficiency of the white race stands confirmed. After Habib Benglia, of whom nobody today contests that he is one of our best actors, here is Féral Benga who has recently been revivifying our all but dead music-hall after the departure of the great black troupe, the Black Birds, whose presence last summer, sadly too brief, disturbed our torpor.

Before *Louisiana*, the American Negro operetta which will probably soon be staged at the Porte Saint-Martin (with Louis Douglas as manager and Strappy Jones in the leading role), and the film *Hallelujah*, which, it is to be hoped will soon be screened in public, it is to Féral Benga that the responsibility falls to represent his admirable race before the Parisian public. He is more than worthy of this, as much for his remarkable beauty as for his talent as a dancer.

BLACK BIRDS.[1] — Pointless to seek any longer an explanation for coloured people suddenly breaking, with an incongruous extravagance, an absurd stutterers' silence: we are rotting away with neurasthenia under our roofs, a cemetery and common grave of so much pathetic rubbish; while the blacks who (in America or elsewhere) are civilised along with us and who, today, dance and cry out, are marshy emanations of the decomposition who are set aflame above this immense cemetery: so, in a vaguely lunar Negro night, we are witnessing an intoxicating dementia of dubious and charming will-o'-

the-wisps, writhing and yelling like bursts of laughter. This definition will spare us any discussion.

BONJOUR BROTHERS. — These two 18th-century ecclesiastics made themselves "commendable by the severity of their morals, by their piety, their charity, and above all their talent for the pulpit," and founded the flagellant sect of the Fareinists, which disappeared in the Revolution.

After their installation at Fareins, "there was talk in the region thereabouts of miracles: a little knife with a red handle of a peculiar construction, of the sort of those described in *La Magie blanche dévoilée* acquired a singular celebrity. The *curé* had thrust it up to the hilt into the leg of a young girl, not only without causing her any harm, but he had cured her of a pain in that place. Some time afterwards a young girl requested the good *curé* to crucify her... as Jesus Christ had been.

"This execution took place in the chapel of the Virgin attached to the church at Fareins, one Friday at three in the afternoon, in the presence of the two *curés*, the *vicaire* Furlay, of Father Caffe, Dominican, and ten or twelve persons of both sexes who numbered among the adepts. These miracles produced the desired effect: they drew to the Bonjour brothers a great number of proselytes, above all girls and women; they would assemble in a barn during the night, without any light, and the priest would gain access by a window. There he would wield the discipline to right and left, without rhyme or reason, and the penitents, far from uttering cries of pain, expressed their satisfaction in cries of joy, calling their fustigator "my little father." Individually, indeed, these fanatics would pursue him into the fields, supplicating him to deal them blows with a stick. They were happy only when their little father had given them a good thrashing, and they avidly sought every occasion for these.

These disorders were interrupted following upon the sudden death of a man who protested against these practices and was found stabbed with a needle. The two priests and the *vicaire* Furlay were locked up or sent into exile. The younger one having meanwhile succeeded in escaping, he took refuge in Paris: the crucified girl and another prophetess came there to rejoin him. He sent the former away in the month of January, barefoot, with five nails driven into each heel; she had spent an entire Lent eating only a round of toast spread with human dung each morning."

(After F. Ozanam, from the *Biographie Universelle* of Michaud and Poujoulat, vol. V, pp. 14-15.)

CAMEL. — "The camel, which seems grotesque to an inhabitant of Paris, is in its place in the desert: it is the denizen of those singular localities, so much so that it pines away if transported elsewhere; it belongs there by virtue of its form, its colour, its

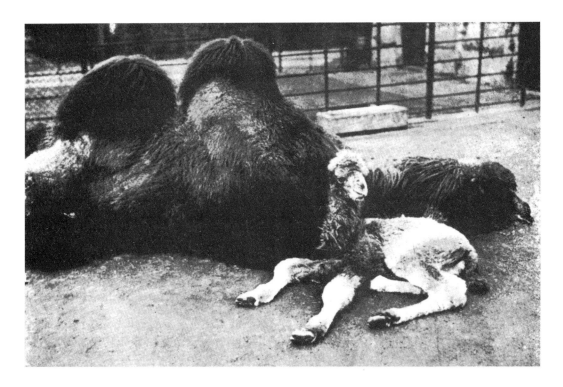

bearing. The Orientals call it the ship of the desert. Launched across oceans of sand, it traverses them at its regular and silent pace as a ship ploughs through the waves of the sea. What would our lovely women say of those oriental poems in which the harmonious movements of the betrothed are compared to the measured pace of a she-camel?"

Contrary to the opinion of Eugène Delacroix (*Etudes esthétiques*, Paris, 1923, p. 40), among the forms symptomatic of stupidity, that of the camel, probably the most monumental, seems also the most disastrous. The aspect of the camel reveals, at the same time as the profound absurdity of animal nature, the cataclysmic and fallen nature of that absurdity and stupidity. One might, indeed, believe that the camel is something that is at the most critical point of all life, where futility is at its most distressing.

CRUSTACEANS. — One day, Gérard de Nerval went for a stroll in the gardens of the Palais-Royal with a living lobster on a leash. The idlers crowded round him, flabbergasted and roaring with laughter at the strange retinue. One of his friends having asked him why he was making such a fool of himself, Nerval replied: "But what are you

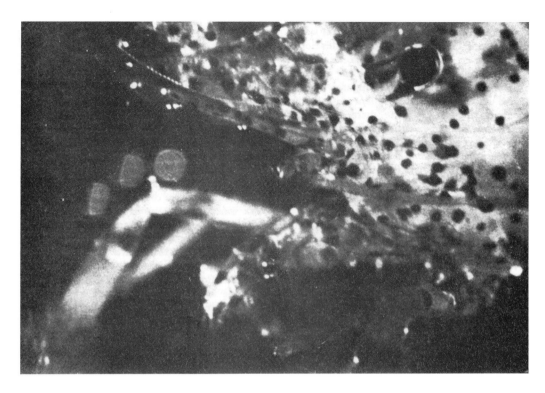

From a film by Jean Painlevé (1929). This page: the head of a shrimp. Next page: the head of a crab.

laughing at? You people go about readily enough with dogs, cats and other noisy and dirty domestic animals. My lobster is a gentle animal, affable and clean, and he is at least familiar with the wonders of the deeps!"

A painter friend of mine said one day that if a grasshopper were the size of a lion it would be the most beautiful animal in the world. How true that would be of a giant crayfish, a crab enormous as a house, and a shrimp as tall as a tree! Crustaceans, fabulous creatures that amaze children playing on beaches, submarine vampires nourished on corpses and refuse. Heavy and light, ironic and grotesque, animals made of silence and of weight.

Of all the ridiculous actions men take upon themselves, none is more so than shrimping. Everybody has seen that elderly gentleman, bearded and red-faced, a white *piqué* hat on his head, wearing an alpaca jacket, his trousers rolled up to his thighs, a wicker basket on his belly, his shrimping-net at the ready, hunting shrimps in a rock-pool for his dinner. Woe betide the poor shrimp that lets itself be caught! In desperation she wriggles, she slides, she flutters in the triumphant fingers. Elastic animal flower, graceful and lively as mercury, petal separated from the great bouquet of the waves. She is also a woman. Who has not heard of

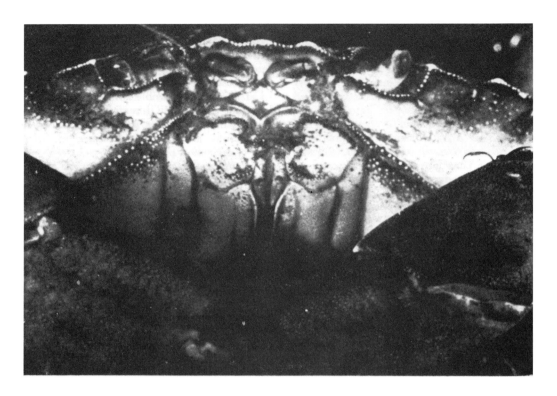

La Môme Crevette?

Among crustaceans, the crab known as the "sleeper," the image of eternal sleep, is the most mysterious, the most deceitful, the shiftiest. It hides under rocks and its mobile eyes watch for passing prey with a cruel malice. It walks sideways. It combines every fault. There are men who resemble it.

The crayfish and the lobster are nobles. They are cultivated like oysters and tulips. They are present at all human ceremonies: political banquets, wedding breakfasts and wakes.

All these beasts change their carapaces, grow old, harden, make love and die. We do not know whether they suffer or if they have ideas concerning ethics and the organisation of societies. According to Jarry it would appear that a lobster fell in love with a can of corned beef...[2]

Crustaceans are boiled alive to conserve the succulence of their flesh.

CULTS. — Los Angeles, 6 October. — Police carrying out a search of the cellar of a house in which was practised one of the mysterious cults so widespread in the city discovered the body in a hermetically sealed chest, alongside the bodies of seven small dogs.

condemned to death and approached by the chaplain an instant before the blade's descent: he dismissed the clergyman by enucleating himself and presenting him with the merry gift of his torn-out eye, *because this eye was made of glass.*

3. Evil Eye.— The eye, be it strange, vague, or simply beautiful, has always been, and still is, among the civilised as among the primitives, the doorway for evil influences. Hypnotism is the culminating point of a phenomenon which has lesser degrees, such as the gaze of desire, the curious gaze, or simply the vague gaze that settles on nothing.

In all these degrees, the primitive fears it, and we might say that for him every eye is evil. He fears the eyes of all animals, above all those that are round and fixed; he is in still greater terror of the human eye.

These ancient beliefs have survived in our civilisations. They have crept into our ordinary language. We speak of "piercing eyes," of "eyes like pistols," of "devouring with one's eyes." It would be easy to compile a dictionary of expressions concerned with the magic of the eyes, the stereotyped phraseology of our run-of-the-mill novels and our best poems.

To look at an object with desire is to appropriate it, to enjoy it. To desire is to pollute; to desire is to take, and the primitive who has noticed a gaze on a possession of his immediately makes a gift of it, as if it were dangerous for him to keep it any longer, as if the gaze had deposited in the object a force ready to come into play against any stranger.

This gift, this abandonment, is above all prophylactic: it banishes a cause of misfortune, and it is to some extent thus that we must explain the majority of gifts made by indigenous peoples.

The power of the eye is so strong that it is dangerous even when mere curiosity animates it: as a result of being stared at by a number of soldiers, Antoine d'Abadie (*Douze ans dans Haute Éthiopie*, p. 205), had a woman who loved him rush to him and cover him with her robe, crying: "Your accursed eyes will pierce me before seeing him." Yet the soldiers'

Drawing of the evil eye on an Ethiopian amulet.

curiosity was benevolent.

By ascertaining the power of an eye without evil intent, one can gain an idea of the power it wields when it expresses an evil desire. One is not surprised that it "eats the hearts of humans and the insides of cucumbers" (Mignes, *Sciences occultes*, II, 879), that it dries up cows' udders and kills little children.

It is essential, then, to defend oneself and, for this, men have found many techniques. The commonest consists of an amulet worn round the neck, representing one or two eyes. Magical formulae, written *medicines* — in magic, the utterance or the putting into words of a formula is itself efficacious — surround the figure; they form, as it were a solvent containing the evil — a vaccine compounded with the dead bacillus — and wearing this remedy amounts to inoculating oneself with the evil influence, thus giving immunity.

Another means employed in the majority of African countries is the bucrane.[6] This, in effect, is the symbol of a powerful defence: it recalls the halting of the animal by a wild beast dropping on its head from a branch.

A bucrane stuck on a post in a field, in a tree heavy with fruit, on a millstone — our scarecrows have not been conceived only for sparrows, which disregard them — or set above a threshold — the idea of making it a decorative motif came later — is the best fluid-conductor. Its whiteness, the result of vermin and the sun, will at first sight draw the eye of the passer-by or the visitor. It will capture this gaze, the first being the most dangerous — and here it seems right and proper to conjure up all the magic of *the first time* — it will suck it in through the two holes of the empty sockets, leaving the eye, that stone-shattering lightning, like a flat battery.

One might, I believe, class under the same heading a "para-eye" I have observed on the shores of the Red Sea, at Port Sudan. It consists of the skeleton of a fish, probably of an acanthopterous or spiny species, its head impaled on a cane switch thrust into a palisade. In the living creature there is a sort of horn over each eye. On the other hand, its vaguely phallic appearance has not, perhaps, been without influence in determining the choice; the phallus, in fact, plays a considerable role in the prophylaxis of the evil eye (Otto Jahn, *Böse Blick*). But this is another question, far too extensive to expound upon here.

4. The Eye at the Académie Française. — The *Académie*, presided over by M. Abel Hermant, has carried out revisions upon the expressions: *mauvais œil*, evil eye, *œil de perdix*, soft corn between the toes, *œil pour œil*, an eye for an eye, *tape à l'œil*, flashy, showy, etc. It has rejected as being unduly colloquial the expression *faire de l'œil*, to ogle, to wink.

Janet Flynn, whose next
stage appearance is in a
French version of *New Moon*
at the Théâtre du Châtelet.

FACTORY CHIMNEY. — When I review my own memories, it seems that for our generation, out of all the world's various objects glimpsed in early childhood, the most fear-inspiring architectural form was by no means the church, however monstrous, but rather large factory chimneys, true channels of communication between the ominously dull, threatening sky and the muddy, stinking earth surrounding the textile and dye factories.

Today, when the truly wretched aesthete, at a loss for objects of admiration, has invented the contemptible "beauty" of the factory, the dire filth of those enormous tentacles appears all the more revolting; the rain puddles at their feet, the empty lots, the black smoke half-beaten down by the wind, the piles of slag and dross are the sole true attributes of those gods of a sewer Olympus. I was not hallucinating when, as a terrified child, I discerned in those giant scarecrows, which both excited me to the point of anguish and made me run sometimes for my life, the presence of a fearful rage. That rage would, I sensed, later become my own, giving meaning to everything spoiling within my own head and to all that which, in civilised states, looms up like carrion in a nightmare. I am, of course, not unaware that for most people the factory chimney is merely the sign of mankind's labour, and never the terrible projection of that nightmare which develops obscurely, like a cancer, within mankind. Obviously one does not, as a rule, continue to focus on that which is seen as the revelation of a state of violence for which one bears some responsibility. This childish or untutored way of seeing is replaced by a knowing vision which allows one to take a factory chimney for a stone construction forming a pipe for the evacuation of smoke high into the air — which is to say, for an abstraction. Now, the only possible reason for the present dictionary is precisely to demonstrate the error of that sort of definition.

It should be stressed, for example, that a chimney is only very tentatively of a wholly mechanical order. Hardly has it risen towards the first covering cloud, hardly has the smoke coiled round within its throat, than it has already become the oracle of all that is most violent in our present-day world, and this for the same reason, really, as each grimace of the pavement's mud or of the human face, as each part of an immense unrest whose order is that of a dream, or as the hairy, inexplicable muzzle of a dog. That is why, when placing it in a dictionary, it is more logical to call upon the little boy, the terrified witness of the birth of that image of the immense and sinister convulsions in which his whole life will unfold, rather than the technician, who is necessarily blind.

FORMLESS. — A dictionary would begin as of the moment when it no longer provided the meanings of words but their tasks. In this way *formless* is not only an adjective having such and such a meaning, but a term serving to declassify, requiring in general that every thing should have a form. What it designates does not, in any sense whatever, possess rights, and everywhere gets crushed like a spider or an earthworm. For academics to be satisfied, it would be necessary, in effect, for the universe to take on a form. The whole of philosophy has no other aim; it is a question of fitting what exists into a frock-coat, a mathematical frock-coat. To affirm on the contrary that the universe resembles nothing at all and is only *formless*, amounts to saying that the universe is something akin to a spider or a gob of spittle.

HYGIENE. — The man who rubs his skin with a friction-glove until it is a vivid red, cleans his teeth with an American product, or indeed takes a cold shower after some physical exercise, imagines he is acting with the sole aim of keeping himself in good health, thanks to a properly understood hygiene, the admirable benefit of this century of reason. "*Mens sana in corpore sano,*" say those in favour of Latin tags. Should one prefer the simpler wisdom of railway stations: "He who weighs himself frequently, knows himself well. He who knows himself well, keeps well." He hardly suspects, that clean-shaven man with his neatly combed hair, that he is accomplishing a magical rite, fit to allow him to appear, mace or lance in hand, next to primitive men.

It has long been believed that many of the prescriptions concerning taboos were no more than rules of hygiene in disguise. "Be thou circumcised," "Abstain from eating beans," "Wash your hands with sand":[7] so many commandments that passed for having been invented by wise legislators, anxious to maintain their people in good health. However it seems today that things might be quite the contrary and that our modern hygiene might be a species of taboo, more or less rationalised.

Primitive man, who was not forever washing, was none the worse for that. Cleanliness had no *raison d'être* outside of very limited circumstances, prior to carrying out certain rites, being itself no more than a rite of purification, a wholly moral purification, addressing itself to exclusively mystical forces.

What clearly demonstrates the ritual, and consequently moral, nature of our practices of cleanliness is the contempt clean people have for dirty people. A man who does not wash is taken by the former for a genuinely inferior being, if not immoral. There is something essentially religious in cleanliness and, in the last analysis, the disdain of the bourgeois for the worker rests, even more than on the difference in culture, on the difference in cleanliness. A *coarse mind, coarse language*, means a *dirty mind, dirty language*. On the scale of metaphysical values, matter is situated lower than mind, solely because it is dirtier. And this disgust at dirtiness can be explained in no other way than by the antique and magical notion of impurity. Evil odours attract evil spirits. One protects oneself from these by breathing in the incense of temples and churches; by avoiding, on the other hand, contact with those who eat garlic-sausage or have smelly feet...

In our time, now that religious values find themselves on the decline, religions, to save themselves, are increasingly tending to merge with hygiene. The Salvation Army, temperance societies, the leagues against public immorality, the benevolent societies, so many organisations of a religious origin whose real aim is to create a *mystique of hygiene*. That's how the fast-one gets pulled: the workers' sole ambition is now to have a bathroom; those who are clean can go on believing they are the pure in heart, and the world goes on turning. And, since there are no crimes, errors or weaknesses other than against sacrosanct hygiene (to kill a man, is that not, in the gravest way, to violate his "hygiene"?), everybody will soon be moral, thanks to Cadum soap, self-aware, thanks to Pink Pills, the enemies of pallor, powerful and strong because their ancestors of genius have invented antiseptics, medicinal mint-spirit and mains-drainage...

JU-JU. — Europeans have a marked predilection for striking and compressed turns of phrase and expressions whose convenience does not trouble their habits of thought.

Thus the first Portuguese who were fortunate enough to travel around the coastline of Africa, finding themselves confronted with the immense problems of beliefs, mysteries, forces, gods, and evil spirits, resolved them immediately, and with a single word: *Djoudjou.*

By the application of the law of least effort, the successors of the Portuguese took up the term; and the successors of the successors were most careful to leave well alone. After a while the Africans themselves made no bones about understanding it. Likewise the little clan of informed aesthetes, who inscribe it in their catalogues in the form ju-ju — which is fairly ugly when pronounced by an average Parisian, ignorant of phonetic conventions.

Left: the eyes and hair of a doll. Above and below: heads of Brazilian dolls from the collection of the *Musée d'Ethnographie du Trocadéro.*

The word *djoudjou* denotes, in the broadest terms, the gods, beneficent and maleficent, dispensers of justice or decent fellows, of a certain number of African peoples it is pointless to enumerate here if the reader really means to take the trouble to finish reading this article.

From the point of view of ethnography, *djoudjou* is a ridiculous word, but very elegant if we put it in its place, that is to say if we consider it as being no more than a term of African pidgin, or of exhibition-catalogue pidgin.

KALI. — The wife of *Shiva* appears in the Hindu imagination under various names and aspects, such as *Devi* (the goddess), *Durga* (the difficult-of-access), *Kali* (the black one) etc.

In *l'Inde avec les Anglais* (trans. Théo Varlet, pp. 12-18), Katherine Mayo[8] recounts her visit to the great temple of Kali in Calcutta, with the avowed intention of disgusting her readers with an ignoble barbarity. The statue of the goddess in that temple is consistent with the popular image reproduced here. "She is black-faced and sticks out an enormous tongue, filthy with blood. Of her four hands, one holds a human head, dripping blood, the second a knife, the third, extended, pours out blood, the fourth, raised in menace, is empty."

In this temple alone the sacrifices to the goddess reach a figure of a hundred and fifty to two hundred goats daily. The animals are decapitated by the priests with a single blow from a cutlass. "The blood flows over the flagstones," Katherine Mayo relates, "the drums and gongs before the goddess ring out in a frenzy. 'Kali, Kali, Kali,' cry the priests and suppliants in a chorus, and some prostrate themselves face down on the flagstones of the temple. A woman rushes forward and, on all fours, laps up the blood with her tongue ... Half a dozen hairless and mangy dogs, horribly disfigured by nameless diseases, plunge their avid muzzles into the spreading tide of blood."

In Nepal the orgies of blood are, moreover, incomparably more horrible than in the peninsula. At the beginning of the 19th century, two men of high rank were still immolated every twelve years: they were made drunk, their heads were sliced off and the jet of blood directed onto the idols (cf. Sylvain Lévi, *Le Népaul*, vol. II, p. 38). Today they still slit the throats of a great many buffaloes, whose sacrifice is, according to Sylvain Lévi, "an unforgettable nightmare." It consists of making skilful and complicated incisions in such a way as to "allow a torrent of blood to escape, which gushes towards the idol."

The figure quoted for the number of buffaloes immolated in the nine days of the Durga-puja festival in the middle of the 19th century is nine thousand (*op. cit.*, pp. 38-39).

The ancient texts speak not only of the sacrifices of human beings and various domestic animals, but of sacrifices of crocodiles, tigers and lions.

Kali is the goddess of terror, of destruction, of night and of chaos. She is the patroness of cholera, of cemeteries, of thieves and prostitutes. She is represented adorned with a necklace of severed human heads, her belt consists of a fringe of human forearms. She dances on the corpse of her husband Shiva and her tongue, from which the blood of the giant she has just decapitated drips, hangs completely out of her mouth because she is horrified at having lacked respect for the dead giant. Legend tells how her joy at having vanquished the giants raised her to such a degree of exaltation that her dance set the earth shaking and trembling. Attracted by the din, Shiva came running, but since his wife had drunk the blood of the giants, her intoxication prevented her from seeing him: she knocked him off his feet, trod him underfoot, and danced on his corpse.

Rich believers offer her silver forearms, tongues and eyes of gold.

Under the title *Hindu-Mythologie und Kastrations-Komplex* a psychoanalyst homonymous with the creator of the *Jeu lugubre* (the painter S. Dali) has devoted a lengthy study to the goddess Kali: this study, written in English, appeared in German in *Imago* (1927, pp. 160-98).

KEATON (BUSTER). — It is curious to observe, in our civilised societies, men retaining their childhood names. First-communion photographs, those showing us in the form of a baby, flat on our belly among furs, or indeed as well-behaved little boys, placed in the proximity (or not) of a pier-table or a column, make it clear to us that the only unity we truly possess is perhaps that of the name. Was Buster Keaton, as a child, really a phlegmatic individual, such as today we imagine him?

Buster Keaton as a child.

It seems to me that a portrait, even if it dates only from the previous year, is always a mockery. It is never more than a species of cadaver and self alone, by the very fact of its existence, a bewitchment. To drag one's old portraits along in one's wake is to become, as it were, a serpent entangled in its old skins. Better, as often as one can, to change one's name, appearance, occupations, wife, ideas, friends: that is no doubt the only course that permits us, without shame, to tolerate the sight of a photograph showing us as a child, unless we possess — like the Buster Keaton of the films — an inviolable *sang-froid* such that, stiffened like a stake by the sword of humour and, never laughing, we become an axis about which the nonsensical trivialities of shifting events gravitate...

MAN. — *1.* "An eminent English chemist, Dr Charles Henry Maye, set out to establish in a precise manner what man is made of and what is its chemical value. This is the result of his learned researches:

"The bodily fat of a normally constituted man would suffice to manufacture seven cakes of toilet-soap. Enough iron is found in the organism to make a medium-sized nail, and sugar to sweeten a cup of coffee. The phosphorus would provide 2,200 matches. The magnesium would furnish the light needed to take a photograph. In addition, a little potassium and sulphur, but in an unusable quantity.

"These different raw materials, costed at current prices, represent an approximate sum of 25 francs." (*Journal des Débats*, 13 August 1929.)

2. Sir William Earnshaw Cooper, in a book entitled *La Culpabilité sanguinaire de la Chrétienté* (translated by J. Charpentier, Paris, M. Carpenter),[9] gives prominence to the *well known fact* that *not one* of the millions of animals man massacres every year is necessary for his nourishment. In seeking to characterise the *red and hideous bloodstain* on the face of man, he expresses himself thus:

ZURICHTEREI

"...of the millions of animals man massacres..." Silver foxes at the Fur Exhibition, Berlin, 1928.

"If, taking the animals put to death in a single day in all the slaughterhouses of the Christian countries, we set them walking head to tail, with only sufficient space between them that they do not tread on one another, they would stretch in Indian file for 1322 miles — more than thirteen hundred miles of warm, palpitating living bodies, dragged each day, as the years go by, to the Christians' bloody slaughterhouses, so that they might quench their thirst for blood at the red fountain gushing from the veins of their murdered victims...

"A calculation based on very modest figures shows the quantity of blood shed each year in the slaughterhouses of Chicago is more than sufficient to float five transatlantic liners..."

MATERIALISM. — Most materialists, despite wanting to eliminate all spiritual entities, ended up describing an order of things whose hierarchical relations mark it out as specifically idealist. They have situated dead matter at the summit of a conventional hierarchy of diverse types of facts, without realising that in this way they have submitted to an obsession with an *ideal* form of matter, with a form which approaches closer than any other to that which matter *should be*. Dead matter, the pure idea, and God, all in fact answer a question in the same way — perfectly, and as flatly as a docile student in a classroom — a question that can perhaps only be posed by *idealist* philosophers, the question of the essence of things, in other words of exactly the *idea* by means of which things become intelligible. The classical materialists did not really even substitute causation for the *must be* (the *quare* for the *quamobrem*, that is to say, determinism for destiny, the past for the future...). Due to the functional role they unconsciously attributed to the idea of science, their need for external authority in fact placed the *must be* on all appearance. If the principle of things they defined constitutes precisely the stable element that permitted science to acquire an apparently unshakeable position, a veritable divine eternity, this choice cannot be attributed to chance. Most materialists have simply substituted the conformity of dead matter to the idea of science for the religious relations earlier established between the divinity and his creatures, the one being the *idea* of the others.

Materialism can be seen as a senile idealism to the extent that it is not immediately founded upon psychological or social facts and not upon abstractions, such as artificially isolated physical phenomena. Thus it is from Freud, among others — rather than from long-dead physicists whose ideas today are remote from their causation —that a representation of matter must be taken. It matters little that the fear of psychological complications (a fear that bears a unique witness to intellectual debility) causes timid souls to see this attitude as an obscure detour or as a return to spiritual values. The time has come, when employing the word materialism, to assign to it the meaning of a direct interpretation, *excluding all idealism*, of raw phenomena, and not of a system founded on the fragmentary elements of an ideological analysis elaborated under the sign of religious relations.

METAMORPHOSIS. — *1. Abyssinian Games* — Wild animals play a leading role in African folklore. The cycle of the hyena is by far the most important in the oral literature.

This animal has gathered to itself all the horror of the pitch-black nights which it fills with its sinister plaints, painstakingly enumerated by the people shut up in their thatched houses, and interpreted in popular divination.

The personification of witchcraft or of the evil eye, the incarnation or the mount of the sorcerer, it is also, on the high plateau of Ethiopia, the bogey man of young and old alike. A game among the Wollo consists of imitating its howls and slowly inserting oneself into doorways, body bent forwards in such a way as to mimic the creature's curious gait — forelegs very long, hindquarters almost scraping the ground — and covered in a white toga fixed to the head by two knots taking the place of the ears.

When, on the contrary, one wishes to make the children and the women laugh, one borrows the form of a good-natured bird whose misadventures are the stuff of legend: the guinea-fowl. To this end one wears a toga, hands joined on a stick, and with one's wrists bound. In this way one obtains a diamond-shaped head, set on a long neck; one's arms, together with the rest of one's body, covered by the cloth. The player goes down on all fours, supported on his elbows, his head pulled in between his shoulders. He lowers and raises his forearms, thus, to a wonderful degree, conveying the to-and-fro movement of a pecking guinea-fowl.

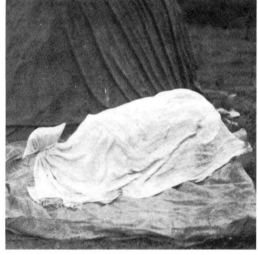

Left: Hyena, below: Guinea-fowl. Photographs by Marcel Griaule.

2. Out of the Self. — Ovid's *Metamorphoses* and Apuleius' novel *The Golden Ass or the Metamorphoses* will always number among the most poetic conceptions of the human mind, by reason of their very basis — that is to say, metamorphosis.

I feel sorry for those who have not, at least once in their lives, dreamt of turning into one or other of the nondescript objects that surround them: a table, a chair, an animal, a tree-trunk, a sheet of paper ... They have no desire to get out of their skins, and this peaceable contentment, untroubled by any curiosity, is a tangible sign of the insupportable bumptiousness that is the most obvious prerogative of the majority of mankind.

To remain at ease with oneself, like wine in a wineskin, is an attitude contrary to all passion, and consequently to everything that is really worthwhile. No doubt that is of a nature to satisfy lovers of stagnant bogs, but in no way those consumed by a higher ambition.

Not to mention the magical artifices that would *really* permit the accomplishment (albeit for a more or less lengthy period) of this metamorphosis, it is certain that nothing counts short of that which is capable of rendering a man genuinely *out of himself*, be it material ingredients or everything in life which, in one way or another, is liable to create a shattering and violent paroxysm.

3. *Wild Animals* — Man's equivocal attitude towards the wild animal is more than usually absurd. Human dignity does exist (it is, apparently, above all suspicion), but not on one's visits to the zoo — as when, for instance, the animals watch the approaching crowds of children tailed by papa-men and mama-women. Man, despite appearances, must know that when he talks of human dignity in the presence of animals, he lies *like a dog*. For in the presence of *illegal* and essentially free beings (the only real *outlaws*) the stupid feeling of practical superiority gives way to a most uneasy envy; in savages, it takes the form of the totem, and it lurks in comic disguise within our grandmothers' feathered hats. There are so many animals in this world, and so much that we have lost! The innocent cruelty; the opaque monstrosity of eyes scarcely distinguishable from the little bubbles that form on the surface of mud; the horror as integral to life as light is to a tree. There remain the office, the identity card, an existence of bitter servitude, and yet, that shrill madness which, in certain deviant states, borders on metamorphosis.

The obsession with *metamorphosis* can be defined as a violent need — *identical, furthermore, with all our animal needs* — that suddenly impels us to cast off the gestures and attitudes requisite to human nature. A man in an apartment, for example, will set to grovelling before those around him and eat dog's food. There is, in every man, an animal thus imprisoned, like a galley slave, and there is a gate, and if we open the gate, the animal will rush out, like the slave finding his way to escape. The man falls dead, and the beast acts as a beast, with no care for the poetic wonder of the dead man. Thus man is seen as a prison of bureaucratic aspect.

METAPHOR. — (From the Greek μεταφορα, a transfer) is "a figure by which the mind applies the name of one object to another, because of a shared characteristic that allows them to be set beside one another and compared." (Darmesteter). Nevertheless, it is hard to know where metaphor begins and ends. An abstract word is formed by the sublimation of a concrete word. A concrete word, which designates an object only by one of its qualities, is itself hardly more than a metaphor, or at the very least a figurative expression. Moreover, to designate an object by an expression to which it corresponds, not figuratively but actually would necessitate knowing the very essence of that object, which is impossible, since we can know only phenomena, not things in themselves.

Not only language, but the whole of intellectual life is based on a game of transpositions, of symbols, which can be described as metaphorical. On the other hand, knowledge always proceeds by comparison, which connects all known objects to one another in relations of interdependency. Given any two among them, it is impossible to determine which is designated by the name proper to it and is not a metaphor of the other, and vice versa. A man is a moving tree, just as much as a tree is a man who has put down roots. In the same way, the sky is a rarefied earth, the earth a denser sky. And if I see a dog running, it is just as much the *run that is dogging*.

Even this article is metaphorical.

MISFORTUNE. — It is beyond doubt that everything has been said, written, printed, cried out or moaned regarding misfortune, only with this reserve, that it is never misfortune itself that speaks but some fortunate prattler in the name of misfortune; which would allow one, furthermore, to make the ignoble accusation that he is speaking of misfortune in the same fashion as if he were speaking of good manners (one would have the dim awareness of being a pompous ass). It would be a matter of speaking, writing, printing, crying out, groaning that vice is a terrifying misfortune, that vice is an underhand and presumptuous abuse of one's wretched person, that vice, in a red robe, is a magistrate or a cardinal, a police-officer rather than a murderer, at all events something that assumes all the sinister and ambiguous trappings of misfortune; which also of course means that misfortune is everything that is hypocritical and mute. Moreover, the streets one likes have an air of misfortune about them, and one only walks along them with the look of a mangy dog. Further on, nobody would be able to say where, or indeed when, anything at all would certainly be possible, that is to say that the enigma posed by misfortune (which does so, all unknowing, to the inspector of police) would find itself subsumed under the form of vice. That is why we so often say: let's not speak of misfortune...

It is of no importance whether or not this be taken for a circumlocution: the fact is that

a certain Crépin, one-time Don Juan and a handsome fellow, who after having killed his mistress and his rival, sought to kill himself with a third blast from his shotgun, lost his nose and his mouth (he moreover lost the power of speech), found himself rebuked by a magistrate for having eaten chocolate *mouth-to-mouth* with Madame Delarche, she whom he was to kill one fine day when he saw red. One is lost in conjecture as to how this infamous phrase from the Assize Court, applied in this context, so faithfully reconstructs the image of vice.

The murderer Crepin on trial at the Court of Assizes

MOUTH. — The mouth is the beginning or, if one prefers, the prow of animals; in the most characteristic cases, it is the most living part, in other words, the most terrifying for neighbouring animals. But man does not have a simple architecture like the beasts, and it is not even possible to say where he begins. In a strict sense, he starts at the top of the skull, but the top of the skull is an insignificant part, incapable of attracting attention and it is the eyes or the forehead that play the significatory role of an animal's jaws.

Among civilised men, the mouth has even lost the relatively prominent character that it still has among primitive men. However, the violent meaning of the mouth is conserved in a latent state: it suddenly regains the upper hand with a literally cannibalistic expression such as *mouth of fire*, applied to the cannons men employ to kill each other. And on important occasions human life is still bestially concentrated in the mouth: fury makes men grind their teeth, terror and atrocious suffering transform the mouth into the organ of rending screams. On this subject it is easy to observe that the overwhelmed individual throws back his head while frenetically stretching his neck so that the mouth becomes, as far as possible, a prolongation of the spinal column, *in other words, it assumes the position it normally occupies in the constitution of animals*. As if explosive impulses were to spurt directly out of the body through the mouth, in the form of screams. This fact simultaneously highlights the importance of the mouth in animal physiology or even psychology, and the general importance of the superior

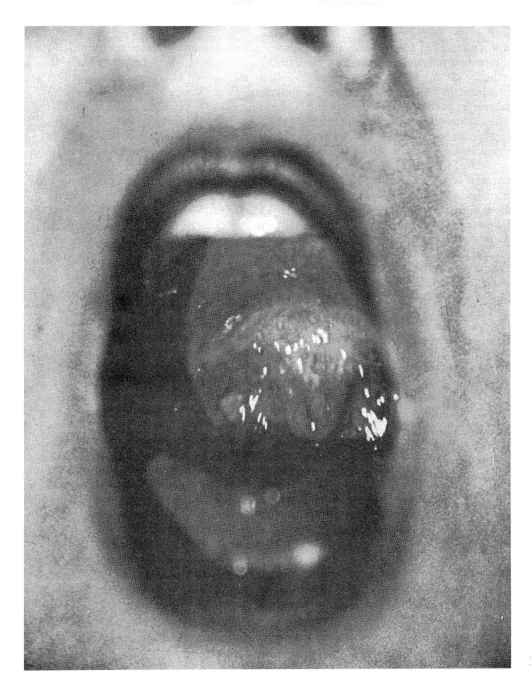

Photograph by Boiffard.

or anterior extremity of the body, the orifice of profound physical impulses: equally one sees that a man is able to liberate these impulses in at least two different ways, in the brain or in the mouth, but that as soon as these impulses become violent, he is obliged to resort to the bestial method of liberation. Whence the narrow constipation of a strictly human attitude, the magisterial look of the face with a *closed mouth*, as beautiful as a safe.

MUSEUM. — According to the *Grande Encyclopédie*, the first museum in the modern sense of the word (that is to say the first public collection) would seem to have been founded on 27 July 1793, in France, by the Convention. The origin of the modern museum would thus be linked to the development of the guillotine. However, the Ashmolean Museum in Oxford, founded at the end of the 17th century, was already a public collection belonging to the University.

The development of museums has plainly surpassed even the most optimistic hopes of the founders. Not only does the totality of the world's museums today represent a colossal accumulation of riches but, above all, the totality of visitors without any doubt represents the most grandiose spectacle of a humanity freed from material cares and dedicated to contemplation.

We must take into account the fact that the galleries and objects of art are no more than a container, the contents of which is formed by the visitors: it is the contents which distinguish a museum from a private collection. A museum is comparable to the lung of a great city: every Sunday the throng flows into the museum, like blood, and leaves it fresh and purified. The pictures are only dead surfaces and it is within the crowd that the play, the flashes, the shimmerings of light technically described by the authorised critics takes place. On Sundays, at five o'clock, at the exit door of the Louvre, it is interesting to admire the torrent of visitors, visibly animated with a desire to be in all things at one with the celestial apparitions with which their eyes are still ravished.

Grandville has schematised the relations between the container and the contained in museums by exaggerating (at the very least, on the face of it) the bonds that are temporarily established between the visited and the visitors. In the same way, when a native of the Ivory Coast places polished stone axes of the Neolithic period in a container filled with water, bathes in the container, and sacrifices chickens to what he believes to be *thunder stones* (fallen from heaven in a thunderclap), he is doing no more than prefiguring the attitude of enthusiasm and profound communion with objects which characterises the visitor to a modern museum.

The museum is a colossal mirror in which man contemplates himself, in short, in all his aspects, finds himself literally admirable and abandons himself to the ecstasy expressed in all the art journals.

J.-J. Grandville, *The Louvre of the Marionettes.*

NIGHTINGALE. — Save in exceptional cases, no reference to a bird is intended. The nightingale is, generally, a platitude, a narcotic, indolent, stupid. With words we designate vague opinions rather than objects; we use words as adornments for our own persons. Words are, for the most part, petrifications which elicit mechanical reactions in us. They are means to power proposed by the wily and the drunken. The nightingale can be classed among the paraphrases of the absolute; it is the senior element among all those techniques of classical seduction in which we resort to the charm of the small. Nobody thinks the nightingale wild or excessively erotic. The nightingale is an eternal prop, star of the lyric repertory, adultery's high point, the good courtesan's comfort: it is the sign of an eternal optimism.

Nightingale can be replaced: a) by rose, b) by breasts, but never by legs, because the nightingale's role is precisely to avoid designating them. The nightingale belongs to the repertory of bourgeois diversions, by which we try to suggest the indecent while skirting it. The nightingale can also be the sign of an erotic fatigue; belonging, in any case, like most words, to the paraphrase, this animal helps to ward off disagreeable elements. The nightingale is an allegory; it is hide-and-seek.

The nightingale is to be classed among those ideals devoid of meaning; it is considered a means of concealment, a moral phenomenon. It is a cheap utopia that obscures misery. The nightingale is to be relegated among the classical still-lifes of lyricism.

It's cowardice that prevents people from using themselves in allegory. Allegory is, in fact, a form of assassination because it disposes of the object, robbing it of its literal meaning. It is defenceless animals, plants, and trees that get used; the weak like to juggle with the whole cosmos and get drunk on stars. Imprecision is the soul's facade, while precision is the sign of threatening and hallucinatory processes against which we defend ourselves with a superstructure of knowledge.

The nightingale helps to avoid thinking and psychic disquiet. It is a means of diversion, an ornamental motif. One attributes to animals, to plants, etc., a moral perfection with which one adorns oneself. Allegories and surrogates must hide the failure and ugliness of man: thus the human soul is made of stars, roses, twilights, etc. — that is to say, one schematises the defenceless world and projects one's idealised ego onto a Chihuahua. One weeps with the nightingale in hope of a good day at the stock exchange. Such is the American's winning sentimentality.

The nightingale outlives the gods, because it is merely allegorical, committing to nothing. Symbols die, but in degenerating, as allegory they pass into eternity. Thus what we call the soul is for the most part a museum of meaningless signs. These signs are hidden behind the façade of actuality.

Poets — those gallivanters and embroiderers — transform the nightingale into turbines, baseball, Buddhism, Taoism, Tchou period, etc.

Mention must be made of the political nightingales, who take their coffee decaffeinated and practise, through Hegel and double-entry book-keeping, a politics of the absolute, gracefully avoiding every danger through manifestos. Song replaces action.

Let us also note that the nightingale sings best after having devoured a weakling.

The nightingale's music conforms to a steady and classical taste; it seeks a guaranteed success. Its cadences are eclectic compilations: only the nuance changes. It even renders slightly daring sounds in a routine harmony, because the nightingale even uses sadness, like pastry. Let us now cite some highly successful nightingales: Mr Shaw, the nightingale of socialism, of common sense and evolution, for whom drama is a compilation of feature articles; Anatole France, the nightingale of Hellenism and saccharine scepticism. And we'll add to the list the scholarly nightingales who engagingly combine the remains of metaphysics with an optimistic biology. The nightingale plays all the flutes of all time; it is more eternal than Apollo, but it cannot master the saxophone.

PENSUM.[10] — Most forms of activity impose themselves on man as pensums, even in the case of activities he appears to have chosen freely. Few painters produce pictures other than by way of pensums, works imposed on them by an alien, and often hateful, hand. How many writers harness themselves to their novel and voluntarily reduce themselves to the rank of plough-horses, or asses, loaded, now with cereals, now with relics. How many people, likewise, enjoy themselves not to enjoy themselves but in order to perform a species of rite...

Everything is hateful when it is done as a pensum. All white-men are failures, for not one of them (or as near as may be not one of them) is really capable of enjoying himself. Leaving aside children who set fire to haystacks, derail trains or dream up great massacres of animals, I know scarcely any but sinister pedants who, chewing on their pen holders, sweat blood and water so as to write out to the bitter end their calamitous pensums...

POTTERY. — Archaeologists and aesthetes are interested in the container and not in what it contains, in the pastoral scenes, the animals on the circumference and not in the milk falling directly from the udder; in the colour of the terracotta and not in the odour it can impart to that milk, the odour of aromatic plants, of smoke, of cowdung, at random according to the cultures of fresh or rancid butter. They will admire the form of a handle, but they will studiously avoid studying the attitude of the drinking man and asking themselves why, among many peoples, it is shameful to drink while

Top: Narza vases, a coastal civilisation of Peru. Bottom left: vase from the Peruvian mountains. Bottom right: vase from Oaxaca, Mexico (both from the collection of the *Musée d'Ethnographie*).

standing up.

Better still, they do not seek to know whether the man who kept the pot in his dwelling did or did not concern himself with leaving the pot empty or filling it, leaving it open or carefully closing it.

They will say that these things are transient and that their reconstruction belongs to the domain of the imagination. But will they deny that they make ample use of imagination when, in a sketch, they extrapolate the feet or neck of a vase of which they have only the bulbous part?

And, moreover, the supposedly preponderant part of that intemperate faculty could be greatly reduced if we were inclined to take the trouble to look round us. There is an infinite field of observation open to the reasonable mind: present-day humanity, whose beliefs, and even techniques regarding pottery have, on the whole, evolved so little since the world began.

For, after all, how many millions of men still believe in omens drawn from pots smashed before marriages or after drinking, empty pots, or those appearing in dreams? Solomon confined genies in vases, the Golden Legend contains stories of demons imprisoned in pots. How numerous are the spirits of Arab magic, still today called *Banu Qamāqim*, the "children of bottles"? How many beautiful jars of red clay, filled with inexhaustible and miracle-working water, do the monks of perpetual adoration see refilled day and night in a certain rite of Christian Africa? And each of them, for its defence, has no less than a dragon, a troop of real serpents, and a forest of century-old trees whose fearsome spirits do not permit even the breaking of a branch.

REPTILES. — A white serpent emerging from the right eye-socket of a skull and re-entering by the left eye-socket — or vice versa — in such a way that its head or the end of its tail are always, one or the other, inside the skull, symbolises for some the eternal destiny of things, the Great Year of the Pythagoreans,[11] the general rhythm of the world with its alternations of dispersion and concentration. One is aware, on the other hand, of the role of the tempter in Genesis and the phallic significance everywhere attached to the serpent.

Left: Louis XIV style vase, Palace of Versailles. Above: Crocodile and Python, India.

In Cairo, in the form of the wooden lizards (or crocodiles?) that many prostitutes hang over their doors by way of an amuletic sign, I have perhaps seen the trace of the crocodile sacred to the Egyptians.

The wriggling of serpents, in the depths of swamps and in dungeons, their strange intertwinings, their combats with fangs, knots or venom will always be the exact image of human existence shot through from top to bottom by death and love.

SKYSCRAPER. — Like everything which has about it a prestige of exoticism, the tall buildings of America lend themselves, with an insolent ease, to the tempting amusement of comparisons. The most immediate is, beyond doubt, that which transforms these edifices into modern *towers of Babel*. But, trivial though such a comparison may be, it is nevertheless of interest (by the very reason of its immediacy) in confirming the psychoanalytic content of the expression "skyscraper."

One of the innumerable versions of the story of the struggle between father and son is the Biblical narrative concerning the erection of the Tower of Babel. As in the myth of the Titans, we find here the attempt to climb up to the sky — that is to say, to dethrone the father, to possess oneself of his virility — followed by the destruction of the rebels: castration of the son by his father, whose rival he is. Furthermore, the coupling, rash though it may be, of these two words, the verb "scrape" on the one hand and, on the other, the substantive "sky," immediately evokes an erotic image in which the building, which scrapes, is a phallus even more explicit than the Tower of Babel, and the sky which is scraped — the

New York: the Empire
State Building under
construction on Fifth
Avenue between 33rd and
34th streets. This will be the
tallest skyscraper in the
Americas.

New York. Centre: The
Chrysler Building Right:
Daily News Building. Left:
New York Central Building.

object of the desire of the said phallus — is the incestuously desired mother, as she is in all attempts at the spoliation of the paternal virility.

To that degree, skyscrapers, the grandiose ornament of North American cities and the instruments of a luxury and comfort as yet unknown in Europe, are marvellous and modern symbols — as much by their name as their form — of one of the most important human constants: that which was the cause of Laius' murder by his son, of the final disaster of Phaeton, indeed of certain social upheavals and a fair number of inventions, the *Oedipus complex* which is, without possible contradiction, one of the most powerful factors in evolution or, if one believes in it, of "progress," since it implies a desire no less for substitution than for joyful demolition.[12]

SLAUGHTERHOUSE — The slaughterhouse is linked to religion in so far as the temples of bygone eras (not to mention those of the Hindus in our own day) served two purposes: they were used both for prayer and for killing. The result (and this judgement is confirmed by the chaotic aspect of present-day slaughterhouses) was certainly a disturbing convergence of the mysteries of myth and the ominous grandeur typical of those places in which blood flows. In America, curiously enough, W. B. Seabrook[13] has expressed an intense regret; observing that the orgiastic life has survived, but that the sacrificial blood is not part of the cocktail mix, he finds present custom insipid. In our time, nevertheless, the slaughterhouse is cursed and quarantined like a plague-ridden ship. Now, the victims of this curse are neither butchers nor beasts, but those same good folk who countenance, by now, only their own unseemliness, an unseemliness commensurate with an unhealthy need of cleanliness, with irascible meanness, and boredom. The curse (terrifying only to those who utter it) leads them to vegetate as far as possible from the slaughterhouse, to exile them- selves, out of propriety, to a flabby world in which nothing fearful remains and in which, subject to the ineradicable obsession of shame, they are reduced to eating cheese.

Photographs of the
abattoirs of La Villette by
Eli Lotar.

...that an ape dressed as a woman is no more than a division of space.

SPACE. — *1. Questions of Propriety.* — It is not surprising that the mere utterance of the word *space* should introduce philosophical protocol. Philosophers, being the masters of ceremony of the abstract universe, have pointed out how space should behave under all circumstances.

Unfortunately space remains a lout, and it is difficult to enumerate what it engenders. It is as discontinuous as it is devious, to the utter despair of its philosopher-papa. I should, moreover, prefer not to refresh the memory of persons who interest themselves, professionally or for the want of something better to do, out of confusion or for a laugh, in the behaviour of that scallywag at odds with society: to wit, how it is that, under our modestly averted eyes, space breaks all obligatory continuity. Without one's being able to say why, it seems that an ape dressed as a woman is no more than a division of space. In reality, the dignity of space is so well established and associated with that of the stars, that it is incongruous to assert that space might become a fish swallowing another. Space will be still more frightfully disappointing when it is said that it takes the form of an ignoble

...space might become a fish swallowing another.

...an ignoble initiation rite practised by some Negroes (Nandi tribe, central Tanganyika).

...the day the walls collapse before the bars of their dungeons. Subsidence of a prison in Columbus, Ohio.

initiation rite practised by some Negroes, desperately absurd, etc...

Space would of course be far better off *doing its duty* and fabricating the philosophical idea in professors' apartments!

Obviously it will never enter anybody's head to lock the professors up in prison *to teach them what space is* (the day, for example, the walls collapse before the bars of their dungeons).

2. Fundamentals of the Duality of Space. — There is no notion more worthy of being cherished than that of space. For that reason it has twice been betrayed: the first time by those who have delivered space over to the geometers, thus reducing it to an abstraction; the second time by the inventors of concrete time, romantics and Bergsonians[14] who, subordinating space to time, under the cover of creative evolution, have initiated the most slipshod spiritualism yet seen.

It is to be hoped that Monsieur Meyerson[15] has definitively put paid to the evolutionist botch-up. We are aware that intelligence proceeds to two distinct operations. Bergson himself said that "our intelligence, as it emerges from the hands of nature, has for its principal object the unorganised solid... For the present manipulation, it is above all necessary for us to take the real object, or the real elements into which we have resolved it, as provisionally definitive and to treat them as so many unities?" On the other hand (the second stage of the intellectual operation), he admitted that "space... a homogeneous and empty medium, infinite and infinitely divisible," is never perceived, "it is only conceived... it is a purely theoretical view." It is by a utilitarian principle that Bergson explains the transition from the first notion of space: solid, discontinuous and concrete, to the second: continuous and abstract extension. If, now, following the opinion of Monsieur Meyerson, we abandon the Bergsonian belief in the primacy of *homo faber* over *homo sapiens*, the two aspects of space appear as profoundly different, one from the other. The first implies an adhesion to a thing, concrete and limited, the reality of the diverse, of the discontinuous, of transitive action by contact or impact; the second, which is nothing other than Cartesian extension, supposes on the contrary the rationality of the real, the logical and icy monism of scientists. The fundamental distinction between these two aspects is strongly demonstrated, not only by epistemology but by the clinical observation of psychiatry. In one of the most important pages of his book on *Schizophrenia*, Dr Eugène Minkowski[16] sets out in parallel the terminal states of the general paralytic and the schizophrenic. The former, in whom the intelligence is ruined, has nevertheless retained the notion of the *I-here-now*; he has retained in an essential form, albeit reduced, some contact with the real. The second, who on the contrary has in no way lost the notion of Cartesian space, who on the contrary is afflicted with a morbid geometrism, has lost the affective notion of the *here-now*, of that concrete and specific present where, as Ward very rightly says, the *here* appears to dominate and condition the *now*.

Thus, *on the one hand*, we conceive rational space as a pure deduction. Cartesian extension could just as easily be called mathematical time. There is no difference in nature between them, but only, perhaps, a different degree of abstraction. If the time, or better, the space-time of mathematicians, appeared historically only after purely spatial infinity, this is only because between concrete duration and abstract time, the sense of touch does not throw across the fragile and perhaps illusory bridge it imposes between the *I-here-now* and abstract extension. *On the other hand* we find ourselves in the presence of a concrete space, anterior to any intellectual datum, and the notion of which survives the ruin of the intelligence. Consulting the observations of Dr Minkowski, and comparing them in particular with Meyersonian theories, we become aware that this purely irrational space is nothing other than individual contact with nature, which science itself, much against its will, by the way, cannot refuse without suicide. At once *syntonic* and *causal*, this concrete space serves equally well as a basis for purely affective pleasure as for purely scientific hypothesis. It introduces the positive notion of an irrational and anti-spiritual reality. But, above all, it can only be imagined as an impact like that of Hume's two marbles: it is the only possible expression of the instantaneous, of the simultaneous, the very idea of which, outside of itself, remains inadmissible. It is the pure violence which escapes time, over which it thus affirms its primacy.

SPITTLE. — *1. Spittle-Soul.* — One can be hit full in the face by a truncheon or an automatic pistol without incurring any dishonour; one can similarly be disfigured by a bowl of vitriol. But one can't accept spittle without shame, whether voluntarily or involuntarily dispatched. This is not, as one might think, a commentary on the kabyl code,[17] but a straightforward rendering of our way of seeing.

For spittle is more than the product of a gland. It must possess a magical nature because, if it bestows ignominy, it is also a miracle-maker: Christ's saliva opened the eyes of the blind, and a mother's "heart's balm" heals the bumps of small children.

Spittle accompanies breath, which can exit the mouth only when permeated with it. Now, breath is soul, so much so that certain peoples have the notion of "the soul before the face," which ceases where breath can no longer be felt. And we say "to breathe one's last," and "pneumatic" really signifies "full of soul."

As in a hive, where the entrance hole glistens from the wax inside, the mouth — magically the body's chief aperture — is humid from the to and fro of the soul, which comes and goes in the form of breath.

Saliva is the deposit of the soul; spittle is soul in movement. We use it to strengthen an action, for protection, to impress one's will on an object, to "sign" a contract, to give life.

Thus, Mohammed himself[18] feared the witches' saliva as they breathed on knots and spat a little to work some evil spells. In Great Russia and elsewhere, to seal an oath, one spits. Just about everywhere, the kiss, this exchange of saliva, is a guarantee of peace (to seal with a kiss). In Oriental Africa, when opening a door that has been long closed, one spits in order to cast out the demon of the empty house.[19] Finally — and this is a startling demonstration of the theory of the spittle-soul — in Occidental Africa, to confer spirit on the child, the grandfather spits into the mouth of his grandchild several days after his birth.

To summarise: from evil will to good will, from insult to miracle, spittle behaves like the soul — balm or filth.

2. Mouth Water. — We are so accustomed to the sight of our fellow creatures that we rarely notice what is monstrous in each of our structural elements. Eroticism releases, ever so slightly, great lightning flashes that, on occasion, reveal to us the true nature of a given organ, suddenly restoring both its whole reality and its hallucinatory force, while simultaneously installing as sovereign goddess the abolition of hierarchies — those hierarchies within which we habitually grade, for better or for worse, the different parts of the body.

Some we place at the top, others at the bottom (according to the value we attach to the different activities controlled by them): eyes at the summit— because they would seem to be admirable lanterns — but the organs of excretion as far down as possible, below any waterline, in the humid vaults of a sea stagnant with distress, poisoned by a million sewers...

Just below the eyes, the mouth occupies a privileged position because it is both locus of speech and respiratory orifice. It is considered the cave where the pact of the kiss is sealed rather than the oily factory of mastication. On the one hand, it requires love to restore to the mouth its mythological function (the mouth is merely a moist and warm grotto garnished nonetheless with the hard stalactites of teeth, and, lurking within its inner reaches, the tongue, that guardian of Lord knows what treasures!). Spittle, on the other hand, casts the mouth in one fell swoop down to the last rung of the organic ladder, lending it a function of ejection even more repugnant than its role as gate through which one stuffs food.

Spittle bears closely on erotic manifestations, because, like love, it plays havoc with the classification of organs. Like the sexual act carried out in broad daylight, it is scandal itself, for it lowers the mouth — which is the visible sign of intelligence — to the level of the most shameful organs, and, subsequently, man in general to the state of those primitive animals which, possessing only one aperture for all their needs — and thereby exempt from that elementary separation between organs of nutrition and secretion (to which would correspond the differentiation between the noble and the ignoble) — are still completely plunged in a sort of diabolical and inextricable chaos. For this reason, spittle represents the height of sacrilege. The divinity of the mouth is daily sullied by it. Indeed, what value can we attach to reason, or for that matter to speech, and consequently to man's presumed dignity, when we consider that, given the identical source of language and spittle, any philosophical discourse can legitimately be figured by the incongruous image of a spluttering orator?

Spittle is finally, through its inconsistency, its indefinite contours, the relative imprecision of its colour, and its humidity, the very symbol of the formless, of the unverifiable, of the non-hierarchized. It is the limp and sticky stumbling block shattering more efficiently than any stone all undertakings that presuppose man to be something — something other than a flabby, bald animal, something other than the spittle of a raving demiurge, splitting his sides at having expectorated such a conceited larva: a comical tadpole puffing itself up into meat insufflated by a demigod.

SUN. — *A form of solar cult in the Hautes-Alpes at the beginning of the 19th century.* — A very singular custom existed, around 1803, in a hamlet in the Hautes-Alpes, called Andrieux, situated on the banks of the Severaire, in the arrondissement of Gap, commune of Guillaume-Perouse. To the south, the high mountains form a sort of barrier which blocks off the sun for a hundred days, between 1 November and 9 February.

In the local language this position on the northern slope of the mountain is called Ubac, as opposed to the Adret, the position on the southern side, continuously exposed to the sun.[20]

In this locality the difference between winter and summer is extremely pronounced. An immense and immobile shadow hangs heavily over the village for the entire winter. The historical festivals, introduced like that of Christmas, by Christianity, festivals about which, under normal circumstances all popular practices gravitate, fade into the background in Andrieux before the more grandiose spectacle imposed by the vagaries of nature.

Here is Ladoucette's description of the festival:[21]

"As soon as the night of 9 February is over and dawn breaks over the summits of the mountains, four shepherds of the hamlet announce the festival to the sound of fifes and trumpets; after having perambulated about the village, they make their way to the house of the oldest inhabitant, who presides over the ceremony and who, in this circumstance, bears the name of the 'venerable;' they take his orders and renew their fanfares, giving all the inhabitants notice to prepare an omelette.

"Everyone then hastens to carry out the orders of the venerable. At ten, everybody, armed with an omelette, makes their way to the square and a deputation, preceded by the shepherds who again play on their rustic instruments, goes to the venerable to tell him that all is ready to begin the festival. Accompanied by the shepherds, the venerable leaves for the meeting-place where he is received with many acclamations by all the inhabitants.

"The venerable takes his place in their midst and, after his having announced the object of the festival, they form a chain and execute a farandole about him, their plates of omelette in their hands.

"The venerable gives the signal to depart. The shepherds, who take the lead, again play on their instruments and they set off, in an admirably orderly manner, to make their way to a stone bridge situated at the entry to the village. Arriving there, each deposits his omelette on the parapets of the bridge and they proceed to a nearby meadow where farandoles are danced until the arrival of the sun.

"As soon as the first rays of sunlight begin to shine, the dancing finishes and each goes to reclaim his omelette, which he offers to the day-star. The old man raises it aloft, bare-headed.

"The venerable immediately announces the departure. They return in the same order as that in which they came; they accompany the venerable to his home, after which each goes back to his family, where they eat the omelette.

The festival lasts all day, and even extends into the night. They come together again towards evening, and many families join together to celebrate."

The role of the shepherds demonstrates the link between this festival and the seasonal life of society.[22] The first rays of the sun indicate the moment they should bring their herds out of the cattle-sheds. The beginning of the summer period also changes the inhabitants' way of living. This festival thus falls into the category of seasonal celebrations; it is distinguished only by the ritual consecrated to the return of the sun, inspired by the particular geographical situation.

The whole ceremony pivots about the ritual of the omelette. Laid on the parapets of the bridge, being the image of the sun, it attracts its likeness while the inhabitants dance in the nearby meadow.

This ritual is completely specific by reason of the latent presence of the notion of the sacred. We recognise here a Christian influence. The sun, and consequently the omelette, are not sacred in the habitual sense. But the venerable raises the omelette aloft *bare-headed*, the sign of a religious act.

The dance too has an efficacious action. They dance only until such time as the sun's rays light up the village.

Then everything resumes its orderly course. The sun has set; all that remains is to feast to one's heart's content. The consumption of the omelette is also a ritual act for, it must not be forgotten, the omelette having been exposed on the parapets of the bridge at the entry to the village, it possesses a portion of the essence of the sun.

The role of the venerable demonstrates the unity of the entire hamlet during the ceremony. The festival of the return of the sun is a public ceremony in which the community participates as a unit.

TALKIE.[23] — After a certain number of sound movies — at least one of which, *Our Dancing Daughters*, will certainly mark an important date in the history of cinema, not so much for technical reasons as because it signals the appearance of a totally new form of sentimentality in films, with the charm of an easy life, unspoiled by any concern other than to show protagonists of a sparkling youth and grace — here at last we have a real talkie, with retorts rebounding back and forth that sometimes add a sort of vocal close-up to the visual close-up.

The English language is the language of *love*, such is the great lesson of *Weary River*, and this is enough to make us forget a scenario of imbecilic puritanism, illuminated only by great gleams of passion now and then pouring out their marvellous reds.

The narrow-minded have not failed in their grubby task with respect to talkies, warning of disaster, like they always do, in this case the end of cinema. Such a film gives the lie to them peremptorily despite its weak-

Betty Compson in the talkie *Weary River.*

nesses, since what saves it is not so much a visual image here or there as the role played by the voices in it. Which shows why talkies are interesting.

Thanks, then, to these talking films, from which we should expect everything (as *Weary River* has demonstrated), we can at last allow ourselves to be possessed body and soul by scenes of ardent sensuality, cast adrift on the raft of voices while everything collapses around us except perhaps, a troubling movement of lip or throat, a trembling of fingertips, an oracular speech issuing from the mouth of an amorous woman, with the heart-rending accent of the mountains, the sea, dimly lit taverns and prison bars at midnight, a beautiful voice, at once harsh and sweet, which has travelled every road, every furrow, every path, in a region where perhaps we know no more about the sun than about the moving barriers of rain.

THRESHOLD.— The threshold is the node which separates two opposing worlds, the interior and the open air, the cold and the warm, the light and the shade. To cross a threshold is thus to traverse a zone of danger where invisible but real battles are fought out.

As long as the door is closed, all is well. To open it is a serious matter: it is to unleash two hordes, one against the other, it is to risk being caught up in the fray. Far from being a convenience, the door is a terrible instrument which must be made use of only knowingly and according to the proper rites, and which must be surrounded by every magical protection.

These precautions are innumerable: a horse-shoe, a consecrated sprig of box-tree, a painting of Saint Sebastian surrounded with formulae, an animal sacrificed on the threshold, corpses of enemies buried standing erect...

In east Africa the most dangerous moment of the day is the opening of the door in the morning. In effect, all night the house has been closed; it has been, as it were, isolated from the world, from the open air, from the cold, from the light. The door has been the thoroughly watertight lock-gate that has dammed up the threshold. One will therefore open it with an infinity of precautions, slowly, keeping behind it, above all avoiding displacing the air. When it is fully open, one will spit into the gaping opening, at the same time pronouncing words of appeasement, and finally, with the greatest calm, one will cross the threshold, looking before oneself.

The same movements are observed by the visitor when he presents himself to the household in the early morning. However he will avoid any complications by not arriving until very late, when the door will already have been opened and contact established.

In superior civilisations the doormat has not been created solely to slow the crossing of the threshold and permit the visitor to collect his thoughts. It plays a far more important role; when the tradesman's representative presents himself at the door of an important client, he wipes his feet all the more ostentatiously on the mat at the door if the house be imposing, and that even in dry weather. Conversely, in muddy weather, it is properly polite to say to an honoured visitor who is endeavouring to remove the mud from his boots: "Oh, I say, please don't bother." The assiduity one employs in freeing the stranger from this obligation is in direct ratio to the respect one has for him.

This goes to show that the threshold, that is to say the doormat, of which it is the visible sign, is indeed a thing of dread, because there one must manifest or cast aside one's qualities, because there it is necessary to register, forcibly or with levity, the rank one occupies in society.

WORK. — "I have no idea what the meaning of work is in our epoch, but I believe virtuosity is an infirmity, knowledge a dangerous asset, and I am well content to have some genius and no talent, which allows me not to work, and to play like a child: Work is an ostentatious thing, ugly and bogus as Justice." — K. Van Dongen.[24]

RELATED TEXTS

from

DOCUMENTS

BIG TOE. — The big toe is the most *human* part of the human body, in the sense that no other element of this body is so differentiated from the corresponding element of the anthropoid ape (chimpanzee, gorilla, orang-utan, or gibbon). This is due to the fact that the ape is tree-dwelling, whereas man moves over the ground without clinging to branches, having become a tree himself, in other words he has raised himself erect in the air like a tree, and is all the more beautiful for the correctness of his erection. Also, the function of the human foot consists in giving a firm foundation to the erection of which man is so proud (the big toe, losing its function as a prehensile hook for gripping branches, flattens itself upon the ground in the same plane as the other toes).

But whatever the role the foot plays in his erection, man, who has a light head, a head raised to the heavens and heavenly things, regards it as spit, on the pretext that he has this foot in the mud.

Although within the body blood flows in equal quantities from high to low and from low to high, there is a preference in favour of that which elevates itself, and human life is erroneously seen as an elevation. The division of the universe into subterranean hell and a perfectly pure heaven is an indelible conception, mud and darkness being the *principles* of evil as light and celestial space are the *principles* of good: with their feet in mud but their heads somewhat approaching the light, men obstinately imagine a tide that will elevate them, never to return, into pure space. Human life requires, in fact, this rage of seeing oneself as a back and forth movement from ordure to the ideal, and from the ideal to ordure, a rage that is easily directed against an organ as *base* as the foot.

The human foot is commonly subjected to grotesque tortures that deform it and make it rachitic. It is stupidly consecrated to corns, calluses, and bunions, and if one takes into account turns of phrase that are only now disappearing, to the most loathsome filthiness: the peasant expression "her hands are as dirty as feet," is no longer as true of the entire human collectivity as it was in the seventeenth century.

The secret terror inspired in man by his foot is one of the explanations for the tendency to conceal, as far as possible, its length and form. Heels of greater or lesser height, according to the sex, alter the low and flat characteristics of the foot.

Furthermore, this disquiet is often confused with sexual uneasiness; this is especially striking among the Chinese, who, having atrophied the feet of women, situate them at the most excessive point of deviance. Even the husband must never see the naked feet of his wife, and it is generally considered incorrect and immoral to look at women's feet. Catholic confessors, adapting themselves to this aberration, ask of their Chinese penitents "if they have not looked at women's feet."

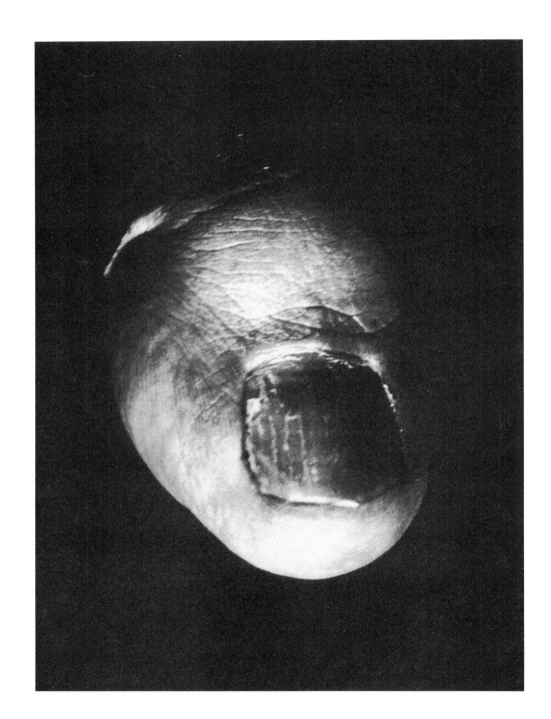

Big toe, male, aged 30.
(Photographs by Jaques-
André Boiffard.)

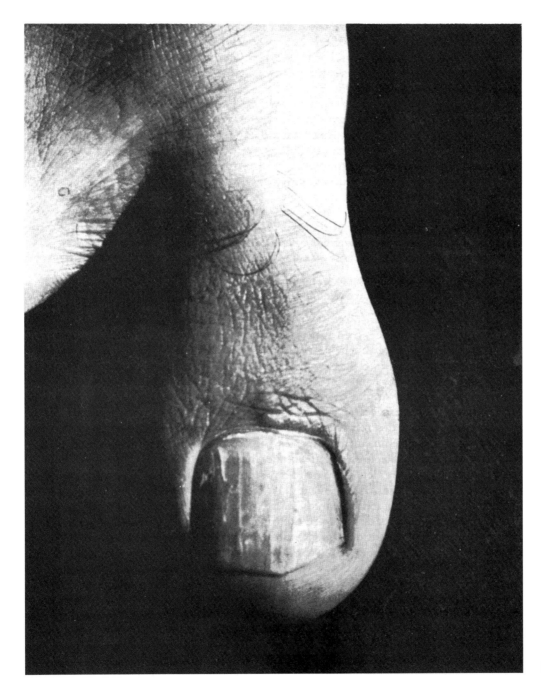

Big toe, male, aged 30.

The same aberration is to be found among the Turks (Volga Turks, Turks of Central Asia), who consider it immoral to show their naked feet and even go to bed in stockings.

Nothing similar can be cited from classical antiquity (except for the use of very high soles in tragedies). The most prudish Roman matrons constantly allowed their naked toes to be seen. On the other hand, modesty concerning the feet became excessively developed in modern times and only began to disappear in the nineteenth century. Salomon Reinach's article *Modest Feet*,[25] presents a detailed study of this development, stressing the role of Spain, where women's feet have been the object of the most distressing anguish and were thus the cause of crimes. Simply allowing the shod foot to be seen, jutting from beneath a skirt, was considered indecent. Under no circumstances was it possible to touch a woman's foot, this familiarity being, with one exception, more grave than any other. Naturally enough, the foot of the queen was the object of the most terrifying prohibition. Thus, according to Mme D'Aulnoy, the Count of Villamediana, being in love with Queen Elizabeth, had the idea of starting a fire in order to have the pleasure of carrying her in his arms: "The whole house, worth 100,000 écus, was more or less destroyed, but he was consoled by the fact that, profiting from so favourable an occasion, he took the sovereign in his arms and carried her down a small staircase. There he partially disrobed her and made free of her favours, and, *something which was particularly remarked upon in this country, he even touched her foot.* A young page saw it and reported it to the king, who took his revenge by killing the count with a pistol shot."

It is possible to see in these obsessions, like M. Reinach, a progressive refinement of modesty that little by little has been able to descend to the calf, the ankle, and the foot. This explanation, in part well founded, is not however sufficient if one wants to account for the hilarity commonly produced by simply imagining *toes*. The play of obsessions and fears, of human necessities and aberrations, is in fact such that fingers have come to signify useful action and firm character, the toes stupefaction and base idiocy. The vicissitudes of organs, the pullulation of stomachs, larynxes, and brains traversing animal species and individuals without number, drags the imagination into its ebb and flow, a path it follows with reluctance due to its hatred of that frenzy to which it is painfully susceptible: of the bloody palpitations of the body. Man is fond of imagining himself to be like the god Neptune, majestically imposing silence upon his own waves: yet the clamorous waves of his viscera, in more or less constant inflation and upheaval, brusquely put an end to his dignity. Blind, yet tranquil and strangely despising his obscure baseness, ready to call to mind the grandeurs of human history, for example when his glance falls upon a monument testifying to the grandeur of his nation, his elation is suddenly pulled up by an atrocious pain in his big toe

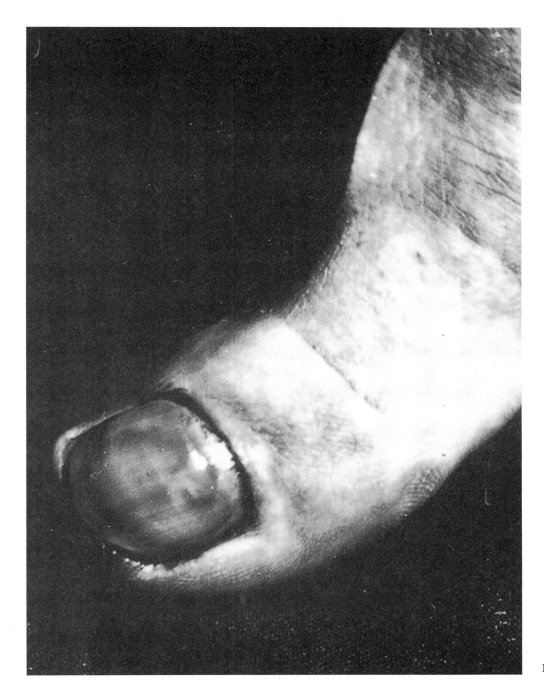

Big toe, female, aged 24.

because, though the most noble of animals, he nevertheless has corns on his feet; in other words, he has feet, and these feet lead an ignoble life, completely independently from him.

Corns on the feet differ from headaches and toothaches by their baseness, and they are invisible because of an ignominy explicable by the mud in which feet are found. Since by its physical attitude the human race distances itself *as much as it can* from terrestrial mud, but, on the other hand, a spasmodic laugh reaches its highest pitch whenever its outburst results in man's own arrogance ending up sprawled in the mud, one can imagine that a toe, always more or less tainted and humiliating, is psychologically analogous to the sudden fall of a man, another way of talking of death. The hideously cadaverous and at the same time loud and defiant appearance of the big toe corresponds to this derision and gives shrill expression to the disorder of the human body, that product of the violent discord of its organs.

The form of the big toe is not, however, specifically monstrous: in this it is different from other parts of the body, the inside of a gaping mouth, for example. Only secondary (but common) deformations have been able to give its ignominy an exceptionally ludicrous value. Now it is most frequently by considering extreme seductiveness that one can account for the ludicrous. But we are led here to distinguish categorically two radically opposed forms of seduction (whose habitual confusion entails the most absurd misunderstandings of language).

If there is a seductive element to be found in the big toe, it is evidently not sufficient to satisfy any exalted aspirations such as, for example, the perfectly unconsidered taste that, in most cases, leads one to prefer elegant and correct forms. On the contrary, if one considers, for example, the case of the Count of Villamediana, one can affirm that the pleasure he had from touching the queen's foot was in direct proportion to the ugliness and infection represented by the *baseness* of the foot, in practice by the most deformed feet. Thus, supposing that the queen's foot was perfectly pretty, his pleasure would still have derived its sacrilegious charm from deformed and muddy feet. Since a queen is *a priori* an *ideal* being, more ethereal than any other, it was human to the point of laceration to touch what in fact was not very different from the stinking foot of an old tramp. Here one submits to a seduction that is radically opposed to that caused by light and ideal beauty: the two orders of seduction are often confused because one constantly moves from one to the other, and, given this back and forth movement, whether it finds its goal in one direction or the other, seduction is all the more vivid when the movement is more brutal.

As for the big toe, classic foot fetishism leading to the licking of toes categorically indicates that it is a base form of seduction, which accounts for the ludicrous value that is more or less always attached to the pleasures condemned by the pure and the superficial.

The meaning of this article lies in its insistence on a direct and explicit questioning of *what is seductive*, without taking into account poetic concoctions that are, ultimately, nothing but a diversion (most human beings are naturally feeble and can only abandon themselves to their instincts when in a poetic haze). A return to reality implies no new acceptances, but indicates that one is seduced basely, without transpositions and to the point of screaming, eyes wide open: open at the prospect of a big toe.

CIVILISATION. — For all that one may dislike proposing metaphors as explanations, civilisation may perhaps be compared not too inaccurately to the thin greenish layer — composed of living magma and miscellaneous detritus — that forms on the surface of calm water and occasionally solidifies into a crust, until broken up by some eddy. All our moral habits and our polite customs, that delightfully coloured cloak that veils the coarseness of our dangerous instincts, all those attractive forms of culture of which we are so proud — since it is thanks to them that we are able to regard ourselves as "civilised" — are ready to disappear at the slightest turbulence, to shatter at the least impact (like the insubstantial mirror of a fingernail whose polish cracks or becomes scratched), allowing our horrifying *savageness* to appear in the interstices, revealed in these fissures just as hell might be in the chasms opened by earthquakes, whose revolutions in the cosmic order sunder the fragile skin of the earth's circumference and momentarily bare the fire at its centre, which melts stone itself in its wicked and violent heat. Not a day passes when we don't notice some premonitory sign of just such a catastrophe, so that although we are not dancing or standing on a volcano nevertheless we can say that our whole life, our very breathing, is in touch with lava flows, craters, geysers, and everything else to do with volcanoes, and, as a consequence, if we hold up to it a mirror with a suitably thick silvering and a sufficiently sensitive surface, it must be capable of tracing vigorous sulphur-coloured lines upon it.

A woman's fingernail, red and pointed as a ruby dagger (surprisingly the blood has remained in the middle and not run to the tip), along with those wounds cut in precious stones by ingenious, hard tools that murder minerals and reduce them to a constellation of angles, murderous in their turn; a bodily attitude that abruptly relaxes; a fleeting gesture as touching as the sudden swell of a sail on a rising sea; these are precious signs that help us understand our closeness to savages, our diverse finery of dark or brilliant fabrics being no different from skin and feather ornaments partially concealing tattoos that depict various mysterious adventures on the body, like the writing in the stars (which offers an aerial forecast of human events...)

We're bored of those utterly insipid theatrical performances uninflated by any potential or actual revolt against that holy "politeness," be it the politeness of the arts, known as "taste"; that of the brain, referred to as "intelligence"; that of everyday life, which we designate by a word that smells as dusty as the bottom of an old drawer: "morality." It would be a mistake to characterise us as *blasé*, but the fact is we're sick of plots that are always the same, derived from our living habits, every day more discredited, and it is no longer adequate for us to act in ways that are identical, for example, to the behaviour of certain savages who think the best possible use for a telegraph pole is to turn it into a poison arrow (because is that not, more or less, what we do when we transform a mask or a statue — originally made for complicated and precise ritual purposes — into a vulgar art object: an infinitely deadlier insult than that paid to European inventions by the afore-mentioned savages, since it attacks a fateful and serious mystical theology and not just mere telegraphy, fruit of a science that can never receive too much scorn?). We have had it with all of that, which is why we would so much like to get closer to our primitive ancestry, why we have so little respect remaining for anything that does not annihilate the succession of centuries in one stroke and put us, stripped naked, in a more immediate and newer world.

For many years the signs of this rebellion in literature and painting have been all too obvious, likewise in the other arts, but so far theatre has hardly been capable of giving us such unadulterated satisfaction, as demonstrated by the following explanatory note, which appears in the programme of a show everyone will recognise as soon as they read it:

PORGY

The subject of the scene is as follows:

"In the Southern States, the land is at sea level and when a Negro dies, if he is not rich enough to be buried in the mountains, he is buried in the swamps where his body floats to the surface again. When a poor negro dies, all the other negroes in the village gather round his coffin and their singing creates a sort of hysteria that inspires the men to theft and the women to sell themselves to whites, so as to raise enough money to bury the deceased. The action is set in a barn."

Pedants are habitually disdainful of everything to do with American negro jazz and art, seeing in their current poularity nothing but a fad, a passing infatuation with certain exotic forms similar to that of yesteryear for gypsy musicians; in short, simply a case of snobbery. Others, more sentimental and lacrymose romantics, speak only of slavery, nostalgia, primitive violence, stammer vaguely about the terrestrial Paradise, or the melancholy of big cities resembling the vast sugar cane plantations with their stands of pipes and chimneys. But now, having seen the *Black Birds* show, we must have done with all this nonsense.

What is beautiful about such art is not its exotic aspect nor even its highly modern content (this modernism is simply coincidental), but the fact that it doesn't really constitute an Art at all. Actually, it seems quite absurd to inflict upon these lucid and spontaneous productions a frightful capitalised word that one should only write with a pen filled with spiders' webs. Obviously, jazz and its derivatives follow their own rules and their own logic, but that does not mean we can talk about "Art," about Great Art, as though we were referring to some particular work by an individual who knew (or believed) he was inspired... Revues like the *Black Birds* take us to a point on the other side of art, to a point of human development at which that bastard son of the illegitimate love of magic and free play, has not yet been hypertrophied.

Furthermore, all this is as remote as it could be from gypsy sentimentality. Negro music does not sing about "the eternal regrets that lacerate our hearts," as they say; in fact quite the opposite, listening to it, we feel a terrible regret, a regret for our painful inability to acheive this sort of simple and beautiful expression, regret for our mediocrity, for living such a mediocre life, so dull and ugly in comparison with these creatures, who are as touching as the trees.

Thus this music and these dances do not linger on the surface, they plunge deep organic roots into us, roots whose thousand ramifications penetrate us; a painful surgery that nevertheless quickens our blood.

What we may deplore in such shows is that, however powerfully they move us, they still fail to overcome our spinelessness and create a hysteria as intense as that described in "Porgy," a hysteria of such intensity that it would immediately induce the audience to commit sordid acts or indulge in extravagant debauches. For this reason it seems the sculptor Giacometti was entirely correct when he remarked one day that the only possible theatre piece would be this: the curtain rises, a fireman comes on stage and shouts "Fire!" the curtain falls, total panic, and the theatre empties in wild disorder.

Some circus acts, like the unforgettable scene in the Gleich Circus when a whole crowd of acrobats performed high above us, perhaps go a little further than other spectacles, because here something real is happening and, just as on the spot where a murder has been committed or in the vicinity of a slaughterhouse, we breathe in the sickening odour of death, that threat of danger suspended above our passive spectators' heads. Really, we are not so far from the Stone Age, and the thick blood of the ancient mammoths killed by our grandfathers often rushes to our heads again in billows of dark malice.

The following passage taken from the *Journal* of 15 August 1929 provides a simple confirmation:

"Mlle Claryse (Diavolina), the new attraction in the Zoological Gardens' free circus, will make her debut today, 15 August, at 4 pm. Her leap from one springboard to another will be 8 metres long and 4 metres high.

"Diavolina will perform her death-leap again at 10 pm. She has been engaged by the Gardens until the end of August, *so that all of Paris will be able to admire this beautiful young woman as she risks her life in each performance of the free circus*, which take place every day at 4 pm and 10 pm."

And so we enjoy seeing other people take risks as we sit comfortably back in our chairs and give ourselves up to the maddening intoxication of danger, while never actually exposing ourselves to the slightest hazard likely to disintegrate our flesh, so much do we wallow in our lazy tranquillity. This is perhaps the only difference between our times and those of the cavemen: today we hire dozens of scapegoats whose task is to perform for us everything we are too cowardly to perform for ourselves. This, I suppose, is the precise reason that murderers are so popular: a beautiful crime is no doubt terrible, but at the same time it is unconsciously satisfying to everyone, and the murderer becomes a kind of sorcerer who has ritually performed the most horrific of sacrifices.

The second quarter of the twentieth century in which we live, is evidently a long way from living up to the hopes of the naïve optimists. Boredom is everywhere, despite these few glimmers of frenzy. The worst misfortune is that, despite being surrounded by magic, we are no longer open enough to the mystical to have the option, each day, to sign the pact with the devil!

GUNSHOT. — The European public, so great and yet so small, has for some time now taken an interest in the productions of the great "primitive" public which it has come to know through auctions at the Hotel Drouot, through private exhibitions, and a few dealers. Some have also been exhibited in national museums. Asia, America, the South Seas, and Africa have been condensed into a few orderly window displays which satisfy this public's imagination.

Inversely.

The great "primitive" public is interested in so-called *aboudjedid* cotton fabrics, in the sixteen-litre oil drums, cheap alcohol, and high-quality weapons generously provided by us. Large stocks of these exist in museums not constructed by this public, in those outposts or "exotic" centres where whites deign to dwell. All of which is none too flattering for Europe, beautiful old Europe with her thousand and one arts, literatures, and industries of high and

Detail of a drum, Ivory Coast.

low price. But that is quite another matter.

From a more elevated viewpoint, the question is whether the naïveté of the black in his indignation over a leaky drum exceeds the white's absurdity in declaring a battle drum impure under the pretext that it's decorated with a man bearing a rifle.

The black is certainly naïve in thinking that anything could ever stop a white colonial from selling him a faulty drum. The height of absurdity is reached, however, when the other party refuses the African the right to "make art" with a European motif, claiming first that it is European — a somewhat amusingly self-castrating remark — and, secondly, that it looks "modern."

One could say that a gun is not a decorative motif. Fine, but such is not the view of the servicemen who outfit trophy rooms, nor that of the neo-Byzantine Ethiopian painters whose fondness for European weapons leads them to adorn King Solomon's honourable warriors with them. And if it took a mere rifle to spoil a work of art, how many paintings and sculptures would one have to destroy? This would not, of course, be tragic, but what an effort!

Furthermore, if a black cannot without debasing himself use an *exotic* element, namely a European one familiar to him, what is one to make of our blind borrowings from an exotic world one of colour about which we must in self-defence declare we know nothing? Shouldn't we then be pulling up the Queen of Sheba, born by a Negro, from the north portal of Chartres Cathedral, or — in a demonstration of methodical rigor — Deir el Bahari's bas-reliefs of Queen Hat-Shep-Sut's expedition to the land of Punt? Wouldn't we also burn the work of Ludolfus, known as Ludolf, who, according to an Ethiopian, drew an exotic sheep while hauling his own cock along in a two-wheeled cart? Shouldn't one, likewise, deny value to the superb spearheads from the Djibouti market, under the pretext that they were made from fish-plates filched from the Franco-Ethiopian railway? And what are we to say of the artistic efforts of the little Galla boys who run alongside trains to snatch up empty Chianti bottles to embellish the pottery rooftops of their houses?

As for the argument of antiquity, only a cellarman could give it any value whatsoever, confusing the part with the whole, antiquity with ethnography.

Boring though it be to repeat it, *ethnography* is interested in both *beauty* and *ugliness*, in the European sense of these absurd words. It is, however, inclined to be suspicious of the beautiful — a rare, and, consequently, a freakish event within a civilisation. It is also self-doubting (because it is a white science, and therefore tainted with prejudice) and will not deny an object aesthetic value because it is either ordinary or mass-produced. Ethnography goes so far as to think that the excessive use of oak in the halls of the Sorbonne signals a peculiar conception of the aesthetic of wood. It considers the pottery of the average bourgeois to be the result of a choice determined by social deformations over thousands of years, as the result of much prior consideration and negotiations with the bourgeois wife, revealing concerns with art that are simple yet honest and, in any case, real.

An informed contradictor might say that I am confusing ethnography with folklore. What of it! I call folklore the ethnography of pretentious peoples, of those colourless peoples whose habitat lies north of a sea of low tides and weak storms, the Mediterranean; the ethnography of those who fear both words and things, who refuse to be called *natives*, and whose dictionaries offer Latin explications of unseemly things, so as to reserve small shameful pleasures for their elites.

HUMAN FACE. — Owing to our presumably insufficient data, we can cite but a single era within which the human form stands out as a senile mockery of everything

A wedding, Seine-et-Marne, 1905.

Left: Mademoiselle de Rigny. Right: Mademoiselle Cécile Sorel.

intense and large conceived by man. The mere sight (in photography) of our predecessors in the occupation of this country now produces, for varying reasons, a burst of loud and raucous laughter; that sight, however, is nonetheless hideous. Upon emerging (as if from the maternal womb) from the dreary chambers in which every last detail, including their rank and musty odour, had been provided for by those vain ghosts, we seem to have spent the greater part of our time in obliterating all traces, even the smallest, of that shameful ancestry. In other places, the souls of the dead pursue isolated country-dwellers, assuming the wretched aspect of decomposing corpses (and if, in the cannibal isles of the South Seas, they go after the living, it is for food). Here, however, the unhappy youth who is consigned to mental solitude confronts at every unexpected moment of rapture the images of his predecessors looming up in tiresome absurdity. Upon our visions of seduction they intrude their contaminating senility, in their comic black mass they submit to exhibition our glimpses of paradise, with Satan cast as stage policeman and the maniac's scream replacing the dancer's *entrechat*.

In this deeply depressing, ghostly clash, every feeling, every desire is implicated, in appearances that are somewhat misleading and with no possibility of simplification. The very

Left: Mademoiselle Langoix of the *Eldorado*. Right: Mademoiselle Boroni in a scene from *Voyage to the Moon*.

fact that one is haunted by ghosts so lacking in savagery trivialises these terrors and this anger. Those seeking a way out have, consequently, always transposed their difficulties somewhat. No decision on these grounds can really suit those who persist in their conception of an order excluding total complicity with all that has gone before, with its extremities of absurdity and vulgarity.

If, on the contrary, we acknowledge the *presence* of an acute perturbation in, let us say, the state of the human mind represented by the sort of provincial wedding photographed twenty-five years ago, then we place ourselves outside established rules in so far as a real negation of the existence of *human nature* is herein implied. Belief in the existence of this nature presupposes the permanence of certain salient qualities, and, in general, of a way of being, in relation to which the group represented in these photographs is monstrous, not aberrant.

Were this a matter of some pathological deterioration — that is to say, an accident that could or should be mitigated — then the human principle would be saved. If, however, in accord with our statement, we regard this group as representing the very principle of mental activity at its most civilised and most violent, and the bridal pair as, let us say, the symbolic

Left: Arlette Molier. Centre: Liane de Pougy. Right: Réjane.

parents of a wild and apocalyptic rebellion, then a juxtaposition of monsters breeding incompatibles would replace the supposed continuity of *our* nature.

It is, furthermore, pointless to exaggerate the importance of this odd decline of reality. It is no more surprising than any other, since the attribution of a *real* character to our surroundings is, as always, a mere indication of that vulgar intellectual voracity to which we owe both Thomist thought and present-day science. We would do well to restrict the sense of this negation, which expresses in particular two non-relations: the disproportion, the absence of common measure among various human entities which is, in a way, one aspect of the general disproportion obtaining between man and nature. This last disproportion has already found some expression in the abstract. It is understood that a presence as irreducible as that of the *self* has no place in an intelligible universe, and that, conversely, this external universe has no place within my self except through the aid of metaphor. But we attribute greater importance to concrete expression of this absence relation. If, indeed, we consider a character chosen at random from the ghosts here presented, then its apparition during the discontinuous series expressed by the notion of the scientific universe (or even, more simply put, at a given point of the infinite space and time of common sense) remains perfectly shocking to the mind; it is as shocking as the appearance of the *self* within the metaphysical whole, or, to return to the concrete, as that of a fly on an orator's nose.

The concrete forms of these disproportions can never be overstressed. It is all too easy to reduce the abstract antinomy of the self and the non-self, the Hegelian dialectic having been expressly conceived for this sort of sleight of hand. It is time that we take note that

Left: Mademoiselle
Geraldine, of the Folies
Bergères. Right: Hélène
Petit in *L'Assommoir*.

rebellion at its most open has been subjected to propositions as superficial as that which claims the absence of relation to be another form of relation.[26] This paradox, borrowed from Hegel, was aimed at making nature enter into the order of the rational; if every contradictory appearance were given as logically deducible, then reason would, by and large, have nothing shocking to conceive. Disproportions would be merely the expression of a logical being which proceeds, in its unfolding, by contradiction. We must recognise the merit of contemporary science in this respect, when it presents the world's original state (and all successive and consequent states) as essentially not subject to proof. The notion of that which is not subject to proof is irreducibly opposed to that of logical contradiction. It is impossible to reduce the appearance of the fly on the orator's nose to the supposed contradiction between the self and the metaphysical whole (for Hegel this fortuitous appearance was simply to be classed as an "imperfection of nature"). If, however, we attribute general value to the undemonstrable character of the universe of science, we may proceed to an operation contrary to that of Hegel and reduce the appearance of the self to that of the fly.

Even admitting the arbitrary character of this last move, which may pass for a merely logical

Left: Zulma Bouffard in *Voyage to the Moon*. Right: Léonie Yahne (one of the performers in Raymond Roussel's *Impressions d'Afrique* at the Théâtre Antoine, 1910).

trivialisation of its converse operation, it is nonetheless true that the expression given the human self toward the end of the last century strangely fits the conception thus advanced. This hallucinating meaning is subjective, no doubt — it appears thus to our eyes — but it requires only that we acknowledge our own interpretation as simply clearer than that of that other time. Human beings of that time, living as Europeans have, in a way that is, of course, obscure, come to assume this madly improbable aspect (the physical transformation was obviously unrelated to conscious decision). This transformation carries with it, nonetheless, the meaning now clear to us. And it is the specific nature, only, of this dated human aspect that is here in question. Certain people encountered today can be seen in exactly this way, but we are dealing in those cases with facts common to all times. It was only until the first years of the nineteenth century that the extravagance of involuntary contradiction and of senile paradox had free rein; since then white men and women have, as we know, tenaciously persisted in their efforts to regain, at last, a *human face*. Those wasp-waisted corsets scattered throughout provincial attics are now the prey of moths and flies, the hunting grounds of spiders. As to the tiny cushions which long served to emphasise those forms of extreme plumpness, they now haunt only the ghastly brains of those greybeards, expiring daily

Top row, left to right:
Johann Strauss, Samary and
Got in *Voyage to the Moon*,
Dartois, M. Godemare.
Second row: M. Kaiser,
Capoul (sporting the haircut
named after him). Centre:
Mounet-Sully in *Amphytrion*.
Third row: M. Marx, M.
Loeb. Bottom row: M.
Molin, Cléo de Mérode,
Madame Grassot, Georges
V, King of Hanover.

beneath their weird grey bowlers, who still dream of flabby torsos strangled in the obsessive play of lace and whalebone. And within the image of the earth's globe seen trampled underfoot by a dazzling American film star in a bathing suit, we may catch the sound, muffled but heady nonetheless, of a cock's crow.

And why blush at that sudden fascination? Why not admit that our few remaining heady dreams are traced by the swift bodies of young American girls? Thus if anything can still draw sobs for all that has just vanished, it is no longer a great singer's beauty, but mere perversity, sordid and deluded. To us, so many strange, merely half-monstrous individuals seem to persist in empty animation, like the jingle of the music box, in innocent vice, libidinous heat, lyrical fumes. So that despite all antithetical obsession, there is absolutely no thought of dispensing with this hateful ugliness, and we will yet catch ourselves some day, eyes suddenly dimmed and brimming with inadmissible tears, running absurdly towards some provincial haunted house, nastier than flies, more vicious, more rank than a hairdresser's shop.

Le
DA COSTA
Encyclopédique

Fascicule VII *Volume* II

-festations that are inexplicable in the context of modern science. The individuals of this group are then the victims of a strange activity. Numerous cases of melanism are to be observed and, from dusk to dawn, the forest is filled with an infernal din. The centre of the cyclone expands with an unimaginable rapidity, sucking up literally all the breathable air. The few specimens afterwards found along the riverside genuinely give the impression, under their multicoloured markings, of having succumbed to a dry asphyxiation rather than drowning. Needless to say, these meteors provide a possible explanation for the body of phenomena.

The inhabitants of the forest's borders, who view the approach of the critical moment with terror, hand down from one generation to the next the most absurd legends concerning this subject, and it might well be said that, since the reports of the first travellers, the question has in no way been clarified. We can draw conclusions only of the most general kind.

Basing himself on an account of Sven Hedin, which is in any case doubtful because at third hand, and on a page written by Seabrook, a novelist-cum-traveller to whose testimony it would be chancy to attribute any scientific value, Professor Prudent has made a rather peculiar remark which none the less arouses more curiosity than the discovery itself: if, on a planisphere (Mercator's projection), one joins in an uninterrupted line all the known points of observation of the phenomenon, after having passed through all these points to the point chosen for the origin of this line, one finds one has described — tip upwards — an ace of hearts.

[ECHECS] CHESS.[28] — Black to play and win.

(Solution 1. ... e5.)

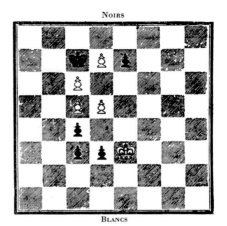

[ECLAT] SPLENDOUR. — *"L'éclat c'est moi,"*[29] proclaims that splendid poster on the walls of Paris, representing a personage in a long, red and curly wig. There are, in fact, behind the walls, vacant lots where the most dazzling acts take place: children's frolics, forbidden loves, murders and rapes, acts which, for each of the individuals who abandon themselves to them, mark the hour of the most vivid splendour.

A being that has splendour and who appears in a public place immediately provokes the clashing together of objects and their breakage. It dazzles, subverts the best-adjusted couples, runs cars into one-another, aborts deals on the point of being completed, makes schoolchildren late, awakens desire and rage in the most resigned. For all that, splendour rarely makes history. Its power of perturbation is latent; the effect is brilliant but rapidly stifled. That which has splendour shines, explodes, bursts into fragments, and everything momentarily returns to the ordered, to the known, in the expectation of the splendour to come.

ECLIPSE. — In the land where the sun perpetually

sets, there is a king of a comparable destiny, appointed to watch over it, and who daily expects death: he believes one night will remain once and for all perennial, and he enquires after the digestion of the toad of the horizon. But he lacks the time to consider the star which, swag-bellied, makes haste into the neighbouring cavern; he has a mirror in his navel which reflects it back. His one diversion is to build a house of cards to which, each morning, he adds a storey, where once a month, the lords of the transpontine isles come in order to conduct an orgy. When the house has too many storeys, the star in its course will crash into it and there will be a considerable cataclysm. But the king has taken good care not to erect it on the plane of the ecliptic. And the house remains balanced in direct ratio to its height.

[ECOLE] SCHOOL. — An establishment where people are taught that it is forbidden to make use of both hands, the left having no right, even when it is more adroit than the right.

[ECONOMIE] ECONOMY. — All moral problems are economic. It is always a matter of whether one should make use of available resources — money, various goods, energy, or simply time — to tomorrow's advantage or that of the present moment.

The principle of poetry is at once that of morality and that of economy: poetry is *in the moment;* an activity linked to caring for the morrow is the only one that cannot be poetic. It is necessary to place the science of poetry at the basis of political economy, for, if the moment came when it would be impossible to augment the sum of the means of production (mining installations, factories, dams, agricultural equipment, cultivated land, means of transport, the work-force), in a word, if we arrived at the point of balance, existing means would have to be *used* — over and above the maintenance of the work-force and the

renewal of plant — for the production of goods that answer to the needs of the moment.

[ECRAN] SCREEN. — Usually a quadrangular surface, material unimportant, stretched over a frame and intended to be interposed between a cause and its effect. A quintessential example of this device is the screen utilised in cinemas. Thanks to the interposed screen no representation of the world ever reaches the viewer. In the lee of such protection the spectator finds himself carefully isolated from any kind of reality or unreality that might be noxious, dangerous even, for himself or for his fellows.

[ECROUELLES] SCROFULA. — Name given by poets to women who are harsh towards their lovers: *De vos cœurs endurcies à nos cœurs trop fideles/ Il n'est qu'un lien, la mort O écrouelles.* [Between your hardened hearts and our too faithful hearts/ There is but one single bond, death, O cruel-ones], CORNEILLE, *Pertharite*, II, 2. The kings of France are reputed to have received from heaven the gift of curing particularly cold women by touch. According to Froissart, curative sessions or *levées d'écrouelles* took place in the shade of an oak-tree at the Hôpital Saint-Louis or, according to Labiche, in the Parc-aux-Cerfs.[30]

[ECTOPLASME] ECTOPLASM. — (ek-to-plasm — there is a tendency in certain circles to pronounce 'plazm,' but this usage is to be discouraged) *n.m.* 1. Part of the human body, external to it, unstable, sometimes soft, occasionally hard, from time to time vaporous, variable in volume, visible only in semi-darkness, making an impression on photographic emulsion, presents to the sense of touch a humid and slippery sensation, leaving in the hand a residue which, when dry, has under microscopic examination the appearance of epithelial cells, without odour or definite taste, in other respects fleeting and transient, whether projected or otherwise, of uncertain temperature, fond of music. 2. Term in statuary art. Work of sculpture in relief or plane, made up of an assembly of gauze, cod-liver and guts, fragments of illustrated magazines, pork-brawn, thread, celluloid collars, *têtes de fromage*, cod's innards, goatee-beards, epiploön, pince-nez ribbons, calves'-pluck, great Frenchmen, boluses, great Francophiles etc.

SYN. There is no known synonym. Fish-and-game-birds' intestines, even inflated with a bicycle-pump, are not ectoplasms.

HOM. *Hectoplasm.* When ectoplasm is manifested inside the body it is called endoplasm. Endoplasms are visible with an endoscope. *The endoplasm of the camel is found at the base of the throat* (Buffon).

TERAT. Certain authors have chosen to see in Rosa an ectoplasm emanating from Josepha, in Radica an ectoplasm of Doodica, in Rita an ectoplasm of Christina. Their argument is based on the remark that the majority of mediums have forenames ending in the letter *a* (Eva, Eusapia). This assertion  is given the lie by the fact that one can cite many Siamese brothers and sisters presenting different endings (Chang and Eng, Simplicio and Lucio, Daisy and Violet, Guarabai and Guangabai, etc.), and numerous mediums whose names do not present the same characteristic (Willy S., Craven A., etc.). Moreover it has been proven that the medium and the ectoplasm do not derive from the same ovum (Dr Baron von Schrenck-Notzing).

LIT. *Les Phénomènes de Matérialisation*, by Juliette Alexandre-Bisson; *L'Etre Subconscient*, by Dr Geley; *Ectoplasme et Andromaque, tragédie en cinq actes et en vers* by John Root and Georg von Kirikaù; *Les Forces inconnues de la Nature* by Camille Flammarion; *Les Phénomènes psychiques* by Dr Maxwell; *Matérialisation Phénomène* by Baron von Schrenck-Notzing; *Der Kampf um die Materialisation-Phenomene* by Baron von Schrenck-Notzing.

HIST. XVIII. CENT. Father Dirag held in his hand the Great Ectoplasm, red and steaming, of Saint Francis (Boyer d'Argens, *Vie de sainte Thérèse la Philosophe*). The ectoplasm of Gernande was abundant, burning-hot and thick as porridge (Marquis de S...). My little sister was very frightened when, for the first time, in the garden, she saw my ectoplasm and started crying, bewailing the fact that she had not one of her own (*Journal de Blondin*, aged 9, cited by Freud). The ballet d'ectoplasmes is one of the high points of metachoreographical art in its purest spatial, patriotic and religious expressions (Andre Levinson, *Compte rendu des Folies Bergères*). Ectoplasmic hammer for thumping visions into the head (*Catalogue de la Manufacture d'Armes et de Cycles de Saint-Etienne*). "The Ectoplasm," a new mechanical leg for war-crippled mediums (*ibid.*). The bleeding nun[31] was, quite simply, an ectoplasm, but far more prestigious and attractive than anything of the sort produced today (Mario Praz, *The Romantic Agony*).

ETYM. Gk. ΕΚΤΟΣ outside, and ΠΛΑΣΜΑ, something moulded.

REM. The exuberant exondance of ectoplasm has sometimes given rise to a belief in exhibitionist ectoparasites. This has been refuted by the best grammarians.

— Greenaway ben Dacosta (the Second)

[EDIFIANT] EDIFYING. — "I love you... I love you!" he murmured, taking our hands in his. How emaciated he was, our great friend! That feeble effort sufficed to exhaust him. His eyes closed again, but his hand firmly gripped my own. And broken words forced themselves to his lips.

What were those words? The mystery of dying moments! They were the very words that had woven the thought of his life and formed the breviary of his activity.

"Kindness," he murmured, "kindness. There must be kindness!... And justice... Justice is not great enough in the world... There is not enough justice..."

Then the words faltered in his mouth, but even in their faltering they bore witness to his constant preoccupation: "Justice... yes... and kindness... there must be... justice... justice ... Justice... in equal proportion with kindness ... Justice..." Then, in a weaker tone: *"Maman!"*

Those were the last words I was to hear from his mouth while, with a still vigorous grip, he continued to hold my hand in his.

— I love you... Kindness... Justice.

Was there ever a testament more noble, more worthy of a great man?

EDUCATION. — To applaud, to exalt revolt in all its forms, and, more particularly, that of the child against its own family; to combat and to deride authority wherever it sets itself up, denouncing its unjustifiable nature, its odious or farcical fruits, especially when this concerns the authority an adult arrogates in the name of experience or age towards a younger person; to hate and despise prison-warders, school-ushers, bullies, preachers, despots, overbearing pedants, police-informers, judges; to emphasise the essential role played in all societies by the myth of the execution of the king,[32] to calculate the disastrous effects of repressive morals, to understand the sinister ends they serve, the accumulation of lies and sordid interests from which they are constituted, to be persuaded that in any case they cannot operate otherwise than in the most inauspicious way and that a person is revealed as worthy of living only in the exact measure that they resist, challenge and break free of them; to pride oneself on having personally broken some shackles; to value one's rebellions, one's defiances, one's refusals; to abominate nothing as greatly as an attitude of submission and obedience and yet, nevertheless, unblushingly to demand this of one's own child as soon as, absurdly, one becomes a parent: such is the disgusting contradiction to be observed at every turn, outside of and within oneself, and the shame of which we can no longer escape.

We do not intend here to resume the familiar trial of the human race, nor to seek in ontology, psychoanalysis or psychology the profound reasons that are never lacking to justify everything. Let our sages spare us their knowing looks, their conniving smiles, their allusions to what they assure us are our limits, the taste they have for our ordure, some because they explain, others because they excuse.

Enough of this complicity in degradation which welds the generations, one with another; enough of tacit understandings, of shameful solutions, of a rendezvous fixed for ultimate common ruination. Enough of this long-term speculation, of this old-age pension-scheme that goes by the name of education. Cease to address, by way of the child that confronts you, the humiliated and degraded man he must finally become. Enough of this "You'll understand later on," and "When you're a grown-up," to the person in whose eyes, at this very moment, and irremediably, you are degrading yourself.

It sometimes happens that one encounters in the street two old people, closely connected, who resemble each other, being father and son or mother and daughter. A strange household; but such is the degree of the triumph of education, since child and parents are in short and in fact joined together and exchange in all equality edifying discourses on their long and intimate experience of the same filthy mire. The son, already decrepit, thanks the father who previously severely corrected him: "It was," he modestly admits, "the means by which you made a man of me."

[EGALISATION] EQUALISATION. — The end-result must be the equalisation of all values. Examples: I. An apple = a serpent. II. To exchange an old-master painting for a bicycle. III. To wear a wreath of table-knives instead of a necklace of fine pearls.

EGALITE (Rue de l'). — 19th arrondissement. Begins at the Rue de la Fraternité (see that word), terminates at 57 Rue Mouzaïa. Continuation of the Rue de la Liberté.

A street neither straight nor horizontal: very pronounced bend at the beginning, fairly steep but regular slope from the Rue de la Fraternité to the Rue Mouzaïa. Length 180 m, width 12 m., paved in stone. On each side a pavement and charming villas. On the left side, going uphill, odd numbers to 33. No. 27 has been divided into two dwellings. On the other side, even numbers to 26. Between Nos. 20 and 24, a wall of dirty red bricks, unnumbered, with a small wooden door, which is locked. At No. 6 "Villa Renaissance." Before the bend in the road is the "Voie du Progrès," to which access by the public is forbidden by a notice, and to vehicles by a stone bollard.

A street totally devoid of interest, were it not for a house:

ANDRE (P.A.)
WINES OF BURGUNDY
OUR SPECIALITY ALOXE-CORTON
PURVEYORS TO DA COSTA
Métro: Danube.

[EGLISE] CHURCH. — A building that attracts blessings in peacetime and missiles in times of war. *They have dared to bomb our churches* — MAURICE BARRÈS & OTTO VON SCHULZ. Also employed as a term to designate a group of individuals, whether religious or otherwise, who meet at fixed times on a pretext that they do not consider entirely futile. It is generally accepted that the very fact of being so constituted causes an increase of vital energy among the faithful — at the expense, however of their lucidity. A fair exchange you might think. They submit to distinct restrictions concerning their external appearance and their conception of time inevitably becomes subject to a characteristic fiction according to which past and future, both grossly over-valued, reduce the present to a simple transition. Between the Golden Age and Paradise the moment is merely an insignificant bridge which one must apologise for having to cross. As for the past, that pile of filth, symbol of centuries of faith, it becomes an object of sentimental regrets and noble sighs; while the future, a shady double-dealer, is all sweetness and light. Each of the faithful sees the church as the opening of a lock which, appropriately enough, takes the form of a basilisk.

[EGOUTS] SEWERS. — Today's urbanists believe sewers represent progress in hygiene attributable to modern science. This is true if we consider only the means employed and their efficacy. But at all times man has had a hostile attitude towards his excreta and waste products and has always sought to be rid of them, and to distance himself from that part of himself he no longer wishes to recognise as his own, that he does not wish to know about. If the sewer manifests itself today in the form of banal and complicated pipework, in former times matters were more sophisticated, and the variety of that which was to be rejected was greater, sacrifices and magic constituting a sort of sewer we no longer know. Man has increasingly sought to reduce that part of himself which disturbs him, at the very least by persuading himself that this is the domain of hygiene. However the result is pretty unconvincing. Luckily insanity, torture and war maintain the complexity of a world in which shit is as indispensable as roses.

EJACULATION. — According to the *Petit Larousse Illustré*, a short prayer uttered with fervour. Its brevity is generally to be deplored, as is its tendency, in certain circles, to be frequently repeated, which is strictly contrary to the express instructions of the Ecclesiastical Authorities. These are thorny questions of conscience which arise for all the faithful, but which artists, writers and financiers have, in their own domains, resolved in terms of the strictest economy.

[ELEGIE] ELEGY. — "How long since you seen Boirot?"

"Boirot, I'll tell you, I see him and I don't see him."

"When it comes to my sister marrying..."

"Your sister, which one?"

"My sister Pauline." (Pronounced Poline.)

"I really should have screwed her."

"Nice of you to say so... Me too."

"When it comes to my sister marrying, there's Ma said to me: 'I want Boirot at the wedding, his mother and me were pregnant together.'

"So then I went round all the brothels in the town.

"And in the last one I finds Boirot.

"I says to him: 'They're marrying off my sister.' "

" 'Your sister, which one?' "

"My sister Pauline."

" 'I really should have screwed her.' "

"Nice of you to say so... Me too."

"Well, there's Ma wants you at the wedding, it's for Wednesday evening at seven.

" 'Wednesday evening, seven. I'll be there for sure.'

"Seven o'clock, no Boirot.

"Quarter past seven, no Boirot. In the corner, the brother of the one who's marrying my sister Pauline says: 'I reckon your mate's late.'

"I reply: 'We'll have to excuse him, maybe he's got the time wrong. Perhaps the swing-bridge on the canal was against him.'

"Half-past seven, no Boirot.

"Quarter to eight, no Boirot.

"Then the feather-merchant from the corner, the brother of the one who's marrying my sister Pauline says: 'Maybe we could sit down to table.'

"Right away, Ma says: 'We won't sit down to table without Boirot. His mother and me were pregnant together.'

"Finally, at eight, Boirot arrives.

"We sit down at table. They sit him beside my sister Pauline.

"At the starters he talks dirty to her.

"At the roast beef he's touching her up.

"At dessert he shoves his hand up her skirt...

"Then the feather-merchant from the corner, the brother of the one who's marrying my sister Pauline says to me: 'I reckon your friend's over-doing it.'

"Me, I says to Boirot: 'I reckon you've made your little impression. Maybe you should make tracks.'

"He says to me: 'You're right, now I can bugger off.'

"I went with him. He said to me: 'You go first.'

"Me, like a good sort, I go first.

"He doesn't give a toss about me.

"Ever since then I don't see Boirot no more."

ELEVATION. — Whilst, in former times, the weaver was subjected to fatiguing toil in working his loom by hand, today he carries out the same work without fatigue and in the same time. Thanks to the electric motor harnessed to his loom, the weaver limits himself to having it watched over by his daughter or his wife, to the great benefit to the manufacture itself as well as to the morals of the working class.

[ELIE] ELIAS. — "The Miracle Child": born 18 August 1792 of the *curé* François Bonjour[33] and one of the two women he had brought with him to Paris, both pregnant by his exertions; he was welcomed as the renewer of the world and, as such, qualified to cleave the Beast in twain: "Elias verily cometh first, and restoreth all things" (J.C.).[34] By him the true chosen people must be constituted, from whom the Catholics shall be set apart and to whom the Jews shall be called, re-established in their ancient faith. The coming of Elie Bonjour was greeted with innumerable hymns of a frankly progressive character:

> La croix n'est-elle pas le lit
> Où l'époux a l'épouse dit:
> Venez, ô ma bien-aimée,
> Venez recevoir la rosée
> Qui doit féconder votre sein.
> Je veux que mon germe divin
> Environne notre hyménée

Is not the cross the bed / Where the husband to the wife says / Come, O my beloved / Come, receive the dew / That must fecundate your womb. / I wish that my divine seed / Shall encompass our nuptials.]

After having promised much, and even given precocious tokens of his divine mission (not having ceased to cry from a week after his birth, he abruptly fell silent on the evening of 2 September, when the massacre of the priests began)[35] Elie, who at his majority, was to have been transfigured into the Holy Spirit, to some extent disappointed the fervour of his faithful by devoting his entire activity to the linen trade and, under Louis-Philippe, sporting the uniform of a colonel of the *Garde Nationale de Paris*. Died 4 September 1866.

[ELOGE, DE LA PERRUQUE] EULOGY (OF THE PERIWIG).— Tragic, without a doubt, was the fate of Monsieur de Fondpierre, who would for all that have been a man of merit had he not been bald. Moreover his baldness, precocious though it

was, would not have been any the less fatal if he had consented to purchase a periwig. Now that the fashion is no more, to be sure slanderous tongues have a good opportunity to make a mockery of it. But, for my part, I greatly regret that the wearing of the periwig should have fallen into desuetude. And I am persuaded that it will suffice for me to recount to you the misfortunes of Monsieur de Fondpierre for you to agree with me completely .

The hair has throughout history been the guarantee of a man's strength, and I do not suppose I need remind you in this connection what Samson's secret was, or that it was under a laurel-crown that Julius Caesar concealed the nudity of his occiput: on the other hand, I am happy to point out to you, in passing, that the periwig was not in universal use in Europe until after it had been adopted by Louis XIV; it is to a French king that the world owes this admirable artifice, and from this it follows that France is the leading nation in the world.

Let us add by way of parenthesis that change might well be the fundamental principle of civi-lised peoples, whereas among barbarians the laws must remain immutable on pain of no longer being respected; among barbarians people are tattooed, religion is of an unexampled severity, they never cut their hair; in France, where an ancient culture is triumphant, doubt reigns, along with freethinking, the black market, financial and political machinations, and the only laws people deign to obey are those promulgated by a code which, when all is said and done, is no more than change established as a divinity.

But, all things considered, if I wish to show you that it is regrettable that the fashion of the periwig should have fallen into desuetude, there is but one way that might be truly striking, and that is to relate — with all the precision one is entitled to expect of a quasi-scientific study — the downfall of Monsieur de Fondpierre, of which mention has already been made: I shall first show how the precocious baldness of which he was the victim was the cause of misfortunes, and then that, if he had worn a periwig, his misfortunes would not have befallen him. (See **Entité**.)

[EMBELLIR] EMBELLISH. — Act of smoothing, regularising, adapting an object to the taste of the greatest number. The object that is beautiful in itself does not exist. It must be voted such.

[EMERAUDE] EMERALD. — Aphanipterous insect, parasite of the Caledonian Wintergreen, a plant peculiar to central Scotland. At times endowed at night with an intermittent phosphorescence which, not touching it at any point, created, above it, parallel to the whole of the individual, a sort of green halo. For as long as this luminous phenomenon persisted, the animal, white in its natural state, appeared, thanks to the reflection of its nimbus, of a rich emerald shade that justified its name.[36]

EMMENAGOGUE (Constantin). — French critic, of Greek extraction, inventor of the rules of prosody.[37]

[ENCLUME, LE SPECTRE DE L'] SPECTRE OF THE ANVIL. — If I did not fear to expose myself to a comparison I have reason to believe would be harmful in my regard, I would willingly walk in the footsteps of the admirable Rivarol; and if I composed, after him, a second eulogy of the French language, I would

certainly not have rested till I had set forth for the admiration of nations the variety and richness of turns of phrase available to the writer concerned for the elegance of his style. None the less, although the torch of my ambition burns low, it is not yet extinguished and, my lack of merit notwithstanding, I flatter myself that I can render an important service to the French language. People today frequently make use of the following expression: *j'ai un spectre d'enclume devant mes yeux* [I see before me the spectre of an anvil]. Marvellous as it is, its origin is not known; which is regrettable since instinct not supported by a degree of erudition does not suffice. Fallen into desuetude after the Revolution, under the fallacious pretext that it was open to change, the expression, if I am not mistaken, owes its return to favour after the war of 1914 to Monsieur Abel Hermant.[38] It there and then knew a great popularity, equal at least to that it enjoyed in the *belle époque*, and it is now in such constant use that I cannot but warn young persons to moderate their enthusiasm for it, for fear that it might lose some of its sparkle by reason of this over-use.

Curious to dissipate the mystery that reigns over the origin of the expression in question, I was quite unsparing in my efforts and, after long years, fate had pity on me and granted that I open the *Mémoires* (published clandestinely in 1713) of the Chevalier de Sainte-Epine, who was one of the most polished courtiers of Louis XIV. Permit me to quote the passage that treats of the object of my curiosity:

"Since we were speaking in the King's presence of the new fountain constructed at Marly by the celebrated architect Monsieur l'Enclume, the fancy took his Majesty to go and see it, albeit that the day was especially hot.

"The waters in the basin of that fountain were intended to serve as the theatre for the graceful and amorous gambols of the royal swans. Only, although the basins of fountains are ordinarily paved with stone, Monsieur l'Enclume had had the witty idea of replacing the stone with silvered glass, with the effect that his basin was in truth a large concave mirror. The uneasiness of the swans when first they were placed in it is readily to be imagined. It is not, even for a swan, an agreeable fate to be haunted without respite by one's own image. What is more, any inclination to escape had been ably anticipated: they were incapable of taking flight; it had been enough to remove from the wings of each of them one or two of those large feathers called quills which are the principal support of the creature in the air. Despondent victims of the illusion the malevolent genius of man had procured them, few indeed were the swans that did not lose their wits; which was a pleasing spectacle, and most suitable, as well one may imagine, to divert a frivolous court, greedy for novelty.

"Chance brought it about that the King, who wished to see the supposed marvel before taking his luncheon, reached the goal of his promenade shortly before noon. A brilliant and numerous company was following him, excited as much by curiosity as by the desire to please. If my memory is not deceiving me, Monsieur, his brother was there, although at that time he was angry with him, since he had lately forbidden him to wear women's dress outside his apartments; likewise present were Monsieur le Prince, la Grande Mademoiselle and Monsieur le Prince de Conti. The King had on his arm Madame de Montespan, then at the height of her favour.

"No doubt I am presuming greatly upon the attention the reader condescends to lend me; but I cannot mention the King's mistress without the desire overtaking me to relate, by way of a parenthesis, an anecdote told me by a valet de chambre attached to the Royal House of France, one which I flatter myself will divert those curious to know how the victor of Namur conducted himself when the eyes of the world were not upon him.

"Cliton (such is the name of the valet to whom I owe the telling of this anecdote) entered one night by mistake the chamber where His Majesty was accustomed to converse alone with Madame de Montespan; he was on the point of withdrawing when he heard the sound of laughter and words that seemed to come from the bed where the couple were: the curtains being drawn, he was not at liberty to observe anything of their frolics, but, by way of recompense, he ran no risk since they could not know, short of leaving the bed, that they were not alone, and that, to all appearances, they had no inclination to do. He has since assured me that it was unwillingly that he allowed curiosity to carry him beyond the bounds of decorum. To tell the truth, his curiosity had barely carried him away when it gave way to prudence; Cliton is not at all courageous, far from it. However that may be, he leant an ear to some of the words His Majesty was exchanging with his favourite. They do not fail to give me a good opinion of his gallantry: when Madame de Montespan cried out that she had no idea of what name it was seemly to give the monster with which her eyes were dazzled, the King, according to what Cliton informed me, contented himself with responding, in the manner of the nymph Echo: Louis. But let us leave it at that; we shall speak of this elsewhere, in the chapter devoted to the King's amours. Let us get back to the point.

"I was saying, then, that chance brought it about that the King came to the goal of his promenade just before noon; thanks to the shade provided by the trees that bordered the way they had taken, none thought to complain of the heat, which none the less was considerable. As you might well imagine, all those present were disappointed when they saw that the fountain was in a clearing bathed in sunlight. For that reason the ladies were hesitant to step over the border of the foliage: and Monsieur, fearful of spoiling the freshness of his complexion, began inveighing against Monsieur l'Enclume, who he said was a crazed eccentric unworthy of his reputation. Nettled, the King responded that it was shameful to be so fastidious, and that he was a disgrace to the Royal House, that he was at liberty not to follow but that, for his part, he was not afraid of the sun. That silenced the complainers, who hastened to follow him. I recall that His Majesty was a couple of paces distant from the fountain when we heard the bells of the neighbouring church ringing. It was as if by their ringing they wished to warn us of the risk we were running; for, hardly had they fallen silent than an extraordinary thing occurred: the basin of the fountain suddenly became blazing with light, as if the sun had fallen into it. The brightness was such that all those present were for the moment deprived of the use of their eyes. As soon as we were recovered, we perceived that the heat produced by the combined brilliancy of the sun and its reflection had meant that all the water had evaporated: at the bottom of the basin lay the swans, cooked to a turn.

"You may have some notion of the agitation into which this event threw our minds. The Grande Mademoiselle in particular who, although she was no longer of an age which passes over follies in silence, did not fail to be uncommonly wild in her utterances, thought to go one better, and held that it would be impious not to recognise how baleful was the omen of which the Court had just been the witness. And Monsieur l'Abbé de Fénélon, since Archbishop of Cambrai, who was then very young, if he showed himself more reasonable, was none the less touched by her discourse. We were the more especially disconcerted that the impression left upon the optic nerve was not so quickly effaced; with the result that, every time one looked down, it was as if a livid blotch were dancing before one.

"Nevertheless, none was more to be pitied than Monsieur de la Rochefoucauld, father of the

present Duc, who lived in close retirement, in a morose solitude, and who showed himself only to the extent that it was necessary that he was not wholly forgotten. You are not unaware that he had all but lost his sight in a bloody encounter that took place during the Fronderie. He would seem to have had his share of ill-fortune. Of this sad fate he made, if I may so express it, a sort of back-handed glory which fitted well with his proud and valetudinarian mien. He claimed that his star had willed it that he should go to Marly precisely on the day the King had the whim to see the new fountain; he added that his eyes were still so delicate that, since the promenade, he suffered more than ever he had done until that time. The King was grieved to learn this and, since he made it plain that he was not at all indifferent, Monsieur de la Rochefoucauld told him that, very far from complaining, he gave thanks to heaven that he had once more been granted the opportunity to remember the forbearance His Majesty had shown in his regard. The King accepted this most graciously and, addressing some young noblemen who were there present, informed them they should be pleased that Monsieur de la Rochefoucauld should provide so fine a lesson in gratitude and politeness. More, he promised him satisfaction, and it was, if I am not mistaken, the next day that the unfortunate l'Enclume, arraigned before judgement, was convicted of the crime of *lèse-majesté*. The Haute-Cour took proceedings, with the result that the fellow soon found himself condemned to the galleys; but, before the sentence was completed, I am told he died of resentment and shame. The King was much distressed at this, but none disputed with him that he was right the better to esteem the tranquillity of a courteous man than the life of a knave.

"A few mischievous wags, to divert themselves at the expense of Monsieur de la Rochefoucauld, whose arrogance they claimed did not impress them, contrived to put it about everywhere that the death of l'Enclume weighed upon his conscience, and that it was of having been the occasion of that death he was complaining when he complained, according to his habit, that his eyes were troubling him. That was certainly by no means agreeable, and in thoroughly suspect taste. Be that as it may, the unfortunate Monsieur de Saintes, who is the son the Maréchal de Bassompierre had by Mademoiselle d'Entragues, and who constantly commits *faux pas*, said to Monsieur de la Rochefoucauld one day when they were dining together at the Hotel de Condé, that the livid blotch of which he was speaking was nothing other than the spectre of l'Enclume, who was haunting him. I doubt whether Monsieur de Saintes intended any harm, and Monsieur de la Rochefoucauld was careful not to harbour any ill-feeling against him. However, the expression impressed a footman present in the hall; it is by no means the case that the wits of a footman should be so lively as those of a person of quality: thus it was that he did not fail to repeat in the kitchens that Monsieur de la Rochefoucauld saw visions, and that he was haunted by a *spectre d'enclume*. It made its way among the common people, who like nothing better than to ridicule persons of merit, to the extent that before very long this expression was very widely used. If ever writers bethink themselves to take as their example the illustrious Malherbe, and go and learn the proper usage of the language among street-porters, I wager it will find its way to Court, for, bizarre as it may be, it does not lack charm."

Without prejudice to the style in which these pages are written — which leaves something to be desired — I find them on the whole most interesting, and instructive. As to the truth of the story, aside from the Chevalier's in no way being suspected of bad faith, I possess a letter which I will be publishing before long, and which I have reason to believe was written by the Cardinal de Retz, in which there is mention of a malady of de la Rochefoucauld; everything indicates that this malady is the same as that occasioned by the spectre of l'Enclume of which the Chevalier speaks. I have nothing to add to this, other than that I am proud to present to the learned public the solution to a problem which has so long occupied them.

EMANCIPATION. — Post-war periods are generally characterised by a certain disorder. Once again we have not failed to experience this. As soon as the Authorities relax their control, murky elements emerge from the shadows where war and the constraints that accompany it have temporarily kept them. That is why we can  unreservedly applaud the measures proposed in the decree of 23 May 1946 to which the National Constituent Assembly, by unanimously ratifying it on the 14th July following, gave the force of law. We are aware that the efficacy of these measures is based on the creation, at short notice, of a new identity-document, the veritable corner-stone of French security, which our legislators have called a *Licence to Live*. Similar measures have been taken in a number of foreign countries following upon a recommendation presented by the French delegation at the plenary session of the U.N.O., so that we may, as of now, foresee the definitive triumph of democracy upon the face of the earth. The *Licence to Live* is, in effect, the culmination of a long series of efforts which have had as their main object the consecration of the inalienable rights of the individual and assure the latter, within the strict limits of his obligations, a liberty none can derogate. Contrary to the monstrous doctrines which totalitarian regimes have sought to make prevail and which the victory of the United Nations, inspired by the spirit of the Atlantic Charter, have once and for all swept away, the principle that has presided over the elaboration of the *Licence to Live* bears the hallmark of a humanism at once generous and clear-sighted, the precious heritage of twenty centuries of Christian civilisation. Delivered, henceforth, from that fear which maintains in men's minds that unwholesome independence which goes hand in hand with the weakening of administrative vigilance, we will at last be at liberty to lend a truly attentive ear to President Roosevelt who, on the eve of his death, adjured us again to "go forward, animated with a powerful and joyful faith."

The Prefecture of Police having been kind enough to provide us with a copy of the *Licence to Live*, which before very long will be made obligatory, we reproduce a facsimile on pages 132-3. Our readers may study it profitably and without further delay prepare themselves for the preliminary tests and checks which will take place throughout France as of the forthcoming 14th of July.

EMULATION. — For us, today, the question of the new English bullets is a matter of painful and quite pressing interest, and the time will come for their renewed appraisal, now that they may well no longer be destined solely for savage populations at war with British civilisation.

We are aware of the alarming rumours that have gone the rounds with regard to small-calibre rifles: it would appear that they are ineffective at killing; they would even seem to be incapable of inflicting serious wounds. An absurd legend, say some. According to others, a harsh reality. Those who have fired the weapon, Frenchmen in Dahomey, Italians in Abyssinia, the English in Chitral, claim they have experienced grave disappointments with their new armament and, very recently, the official American report on the war observes with astonishment the low proportion of fatalities experienced in the U.S. army compared with the number of wounded.

For their part, the riflemen of the polygon[39] view these lamentations with the greatest scepticism. For them, these findings are unduly at variance with those obtained on the firing-grounds of France and Germany in numerous experiments carried out on the corpses of animals. It is not admissible, so they claim, that bullets that readily shatter the bones of oxen and horses should have so little effect on the human body. Besides, to go into the matter in more detail, we recognise that the Italians in Abyssinia were not armed with small-calibre rifles, that many of our troops in Dahomey had the old rifle and finally, that the disappointments of the English in India could well rather be attributed to the imperfections of their Lee-Metford, whose accuracy leaves much to be desired, and also to the emotion of their soldiers, who may not have preserved the coolness necessary to regulate their fire against a fanatical enemy rushing headlong at them with insane temerity. As to the proportion of Americans killed, it does not noticeably differ from that recorded in the course of recent European wars, and it has never been claimed that

them. To cast doubt here upon the reality of his gifts would be quite pointless. Having been capable of being a poet — good or bad — the point is that he decided not in any way to be one.

The Beylism[45] which people have, successively, sought to make a species of positivism, an analytical romanticism, a method of conquest, a flattering complicity, is evidently a dandyism, but a lived dandyism.

For Baudelaire, it is too often forgotten, the Dandy is an other. It is fairly easy to seek to pick a quarrel with him by opposing the aspiration to dandyism, as he advocates it, to the manifest failings in his behaviour. But it is precisely these failings which maintain him in his rank as a poet.

For Stendhal, caught between the ingenious vapidity of the Abbé Dellile[46] and the earliest reactionary and plaintive romanticism, the poetic attitude rapidly becomes untenable. In his eyes every poet is no longer anything other than a solemn imbecile, a courtier like that Racine whom he has come to detest. Besides he despises "charger" rather than "horse." He calls that hypocrisy. Sentimental effusions, though at their beginnings, seemed to him supremely ridiculous. As for "the abominable song of the alexandrine line," he was still one of the few no longer able to tolerate it.

But the time for that poetic revolt, the necessity for which he demonstrated fifty years in advance, had not arrived. His lyricism, always present, always repressed, will be caught out only in brief flashes in the language ("The landscapes were like bows playing on my inmost being"). It will before long slip into the choice of situations. It is here that Stendhal's undertaking inaugurates the essential attitudes of dandyism by dissociating lyricism from words and transferring it, not into acts, which would still be too visible, but to their motivation.

The central theme of Beylism is the secret. Every Stendhalian character (Stendhal included) is reluctant to express his real feelings until the moment when, placed in the presence of the beloved being, he discovers that communication is possible. Love is a secret society, for two.

No sooner, however, are the lovers thrown together, than an irresistible force separates them anew without their being in a position to say everything and, in their pursuit of a happiness fortuitously caught sight of, they thenceforth come up against increasingly insurmountable obstacles. With Stendhal, as with Roussel, the lyrical allusion resides in the complex and irremediable mechanism of an internal plot. Every character, despite the meticulous plans they prepare to take possession of the world through the beloved, is implacably carried away at the very moment when they seem to succeed. Stendhalian love, all the more wildly exalted because it is more clearly doomed to failure, is an outrageous challenge thrown down before plausible reality. Clélia and Fabrice,[47] who come together again without ever seeing one another, but who communicate, accomplish this assault against the night in the most rapturous form.

The poetry of words is not always possible. It is not even certain whether it is always desirable. When it dies of ecstasy in *Télémaque*-style[48] landscapes, in a creamy universe where the storm itself is a sweetmeat, it is then that the anti-poet appears. Not only does Stendhal detest it, he exists against it.

EPICTETE (EPICTETUS). — Stoic philosopher, whose name is broken down as follows:

Pic [pick], curved iron instrument; *Picadae* (woodpeckers), bird of the order of climbers, which pierces the bark of trees; term in the game of *piquet; pique* [peak], summit of a high mountain, etc.

Tête, part of the body which joins the neck to the hairy leather.

E, first and last letter of the name, Epictète.

EPIDOTE. — Angelica of the Far North, devoid of flavour but of an unparalleled hardness. Who will restore to us those windows of spring in the black night? To the confusion of solar souls, although for better times. To *Neptune*, by Le Verrier's penholder telescope. Emblem of passional acrobatics. To be engraved by a porcupine.

[EPORNUFLER] TO EPORNUFLATE. — To seize a patient by the right emfle and emarcillate him in a fixed arstene while keeping the free end of his pelin a short distance from the emorfilator. The verb is also used in the sense of dispersing fallions with blows from a charn.

[EROTIN, L']. — If, obscure as any denuded of their mask, evanescent as venturesome rockets, leaving in memoirs only traces soon dimmed but in other respects astonishingly durable, inexplicably frozen in the set and imperious rictus of defiance, the authors none the less of novels perused with an enthusiasm which, circumspect though it may be, is for all that in no way inferior to that which welcomes immaculate works of genius, there are in the annals of literature certain beings of whom it is permitted to affirm that they are yet more mysterious than those Ancients who only the sword of a legend or the shield of a magnificent death defend against profanation. Such a one was l'Erotin, an enigma among the enigmatic, and whose obscurity appears almost miraculous if we consider that this writer published no less than 71 volumes between 1891 and 1910, not counting 4 works presumed posthumous as well as 7 volumes announced, of which it is unknown whether they ever saw the light of day.

Faithful to the rules of that literature which some think to blacken by calling it pornography — an appellation which, for our part, we are inclined to apply to all literature, since whoever speaks of writing speaks of obscenity — l'Erotin allows himself only occasional psychological digressions, confining himself to descriptions of an erotic nature which specialists praise as much for their exactitude as for their frenzy. There, all strange, lies the glaucous serpent of despair, darting at the nocturnal passer-by in quest of sensual pleasure its tongue of flame, its venomous tongue into the wind, on which, like a sigh, the butterfly of spasm settles. Of literary forms l'Erotin neglects none, whether he chooses the supremely lugubrious mould of the novel-in-letters, that veritable Iron Maiden and, like her, worthy of being exhibited in the museum in Nuremberg or, on the contrary, adopts that, supremely flexible and subtle, of the naturalist novel or theatre, indeed of the social novel. On occasion, carrying to its height the paroxysmal volubility that precipitates the reader into the alternation of systoles and diastoles, while devoting himself, regardless of the most sacred pledges the dreary desolation of balance imposes on the spirit, to the perilous play of prolixity and the deliberate spreading of confusion, l'Erotin exhausts in a single work, albeit of monumental proportions such as *The Epic of Gerando*, the whole rainbow of shared sensual delights, against a background of coruscating and lustrous bronze-tinted palaces.

Not content with dissimulating his identity from the insidious investigations of literary historians, our author delights in throwing even his most faithful readers off the scent, those who, in the closest intimacy of their apartments, have signed in blood and in sperm the diabolical pact concluded between their fervour and the Word, that pact which no blasphemy annuls and which is, properly speaking the condition, unique, whole and supreme, of all poetry. *Pan-pan, Trix, Zéphir, Tip-Tap, Clic-Clic, Bébé, Lena de Maurergard, Fuckwell, A Journalist of the Previous Century, Mercadette,* such are the titles, sometimes not especially fanciful, wherewith he is honoured and whose lack of ostentation one would deplore if, for him, ostentation did not consist precisely in fleeing everything while affirming himself, making himself mischievously elusive while giving rise in the reader to the most haunting of habits.

Raised characters in purple that stand out from the vellum like the silvery arm, adorned with sumptuous veins, of the drowned man on the calm expanses of the ocean; bindings of a poisoned yellow that swallow up the words like the deceptive eddies of the sea, the corpse still adorned with its rings and its memories, with its misfortunes and its pitiful human joys, the waves permit us to gather, just above the surface of the sand, the admirable titles of certain works, which by a miracle escaped the vigilance of the censors, those beacons whose cold light penetrates to their remotest depths the solitudes consecrated to sensual delights: *Her Son's Mistress, The Judge's Widow, The Lover of Young Boys, Mother and Mistress, The Woman Who Liked Dogs, The Power of Petticoats, Man-Eater;* titles about which it is no doubt fitting to have certain reservations as much on account of their frankly vulgar character as of the unhealthy curiosities, forever latent in the inmost being of the stroller, curiosities that the slightest caprices of a thought abstracted from reality can evoke, randomly, for example, on a saunter innocently undertaken, along the ancient *quais*, shaded by age-old oaks, that line the sweetest and most enigmatic of rivers, that which bathes the parapets of Paris.

Let obstinate exegetes, eager to unearth — contrary to unequivocally expressed wishes — the vestiges of a human presence in straitened circumstances, take pleasure in an occupation that inspires in us only contempt. As for us, our pleasure in no way lies in disputing with l'Erotin the privacy in which he so meticulously wrapped himself. The very pseudonym by which we most usually know him seems to us rather significant by reason of the play on words it contains: Erotin, *air hautain* — proud bearing — what a challenge, thrown down at the slovenly rabble of writers who sign their names.

[EROTISME] EROTISM. — Whoever has not chosen obscenity, recognised in obscenity the presence and the shock of poetry, and, more intimately, the elusive brightness of a star, is not worthy to die and their death will extend upon earth the industrious anxiety of priests.

ERRATUM. — Outrage committed against Poetry. Ex.: After having affected an indifference towards poets which some judged to be offensive, the review *Les Temps Modernes* at length published in no. 10 some admirable verses by Monsieur Ollivier Larondde. Sensitive souls were already congratulating themselves on this happy event when they observed with stupefaction that *Les Temps Modernes,* whose high literary tone in other respects was well known (but does this review reserve its best attentions for philosophers?), had presented a scandalously disfigured version of the poem by Monsieur Ollivier Larronde. Judge for yourself:

DEFECTIVE TEXT
At line 13: *Seule une éclipse désaltère l'astre au col*

At line 25: *Du seul poivre la plaie séraphique se gorge*
Finally the signature: *Olivier Laronde*

OFFICIAL TEXT
Seule une éclipse désaltère l'astre au col

Du seul poivre la plaie séraphique sa gorge
Olivier Larronde

One imagines oneself to be dreaming, faced with such crass errors perpetrated at a moment when France, rising painfully from her ruins, dreams of resuming her rank at the head of civilised nations. One thinks with horror of the mortal blow so total a corruption of our literary morals runs the risk of inflicting upon our prestige.

With the utmost good fortune the author's vigilance was not found wanting. He immediately demanded that the poem be published again in its original version, and *Les Temps Modernes*, faced with the vast movement of reprobation to which their conduct gave rise nation-wide, were obliged to do so without delay.

But what is one to conclude from the note that, in no. 13, accompanies the poem at last restored in its entirety, which note, under the pretext of correcting the mistakes committed, sews a confusion which is painful and of a nature to render suspect any future publication? Is this a hoax? a stroke of bad luck? or rather, as we are tempted to believe, an undertaking against poetry?[49]

ERUDITION. — Brief as our survey may be, with all due respect to certain pedants who make a virtue of their prolixity, I have no doubt that it will suffice for our purpose. At the risk of misrepresenting it, whoever chooses the career of arms cannot be exempt from its blemishes, as much physical as moral, that are the shame of our society. And the same goes for religious orders.

The spiritual health of our subject, Anatole de Fondpierre, was in no way inferior to that of his parents and, if no mention has yet been made of the way of life he adopted, that is because it was my desire in the first place that my claim be solidly established: which is that his misfortune had no shameful cause. (See **Entité** and **Etendard**.)

[ESCROCS] CON-MEN. — If, somewhere in the world, someone is buckling down to the work of which we are about to speak, let him abandon it now. Let him, after reading these lines, burn the immense card-index in which, for long years, he has amassed notes and references. At the risk of plunging him into despair, we must warn him that he has in vain imposed upon himself a useless labour. His work is as good as over. A few snips of the scissors and a final corrected proof. In effect, that man, whom we imagine as being engaged in compiling an *Anthology of Human Stupidity*, stands no chance of having found, or of ever finding, anything more stupid, more abject, more emetic than that which has been written about Kafka and his work since people began its exegesis. So let him, without tiring himself, put together a collection of the commentaries of Max Brod, of Klossowski, of Carrive, of Marthe Robert, of Marcel Lecomte, of François Léger, of Groethuysen, and a pack of others whose names I forget. I guarantee to him that, in a minimum of pages and under a delightfully appropriate title, he will have brought together the maximum of texts representative of the most stupid infamy that can be dreamed of. And, on top of that, at the moment I am giving him this valuable advice: we are not unaware of the nature of the play, extracted by Monsieur André Barrault from *The Trial*, the play Monsieur Jean-Louis Gide proposes to offer in the near future as a spectacle for the smart and literate public of the Théâtre des Ecuries Mondaines. But in that connection too all hopes are permitted. The illustrations to the American edition of *The Trial* (the work of a certain Georg Salter, who it would be unjust not to cite in our roll of honour) would seem to afford us a glimpse of what to expect, as if we did not already know perfectly well. Alas the days of explosive rages seem to have passed, and there will be nobody at the first night of *The Trial* to rain down from the gods onto the intellectuals in the stalls a flotilla of leaflets printed with this necessary warning: *It is forbidden to deposit rubbish on the Kafka.*[50]

Ah, what a shame there is no God! With what fervour should I have thanked him for making Lewis Carroll untranslatable and Roussel frankly insufferable! How sweet it is to think that Madame Marthe Robert will never turn her attention, with that erudition which complements her powerful philosophical culture, to the Jabberwock or the "patter-songs" of Furdet,[51] to extract therefrom the Kierkegaardian marrow. It is always tiresome and untidy having pigs in one's salon, but to see Madame Marthe Robert counting the hairs on the beast of the synagogue is downright revolting.[52]

All the more so since we never asked anything from any of these louts! The ineffable Max Brod didn't burn Kafka's works. Splendid. Thanks very much. But that, it seems, gives him the right to hold back until such time as he sees fit to release them, some unfinished chapters of *The Trial*, to remove two from *Amerika*, and, at a pinch, to allow himself a few minor adjustments wherever he deems them necessary. And imagine it: this cretin (beside whom Dr Watson, the total moron who served as Eckermann to Sherlock Holmes, appears as a genius of the rarest and most distinguished sort) was given the privilege of sharing in the life of Kafka! And without understanding a thing! A striking feat. But, all the same, we owe a debt of gratitude to Max Brod for an eloquent admission. He has betrayed himself, the bastard, and, in advance, has set a cattle-brand on all those, himself among them, who were going to fall upon Kafka so as to tear him apart for personal and shameful reasons. Read the phrase in parentheses carefully, and never forget it:

MAX BROD — *Postface* to *The Trial*, Gallimard edition, p. 275, l. 21, here it is: *(without ever having said it)*.

And here is the whole sentence in which it occurs:

If however he disowned his work, this was firstly because of certain sorrows which impelled him to self-destruction and encouraged in him nihilism in matters of publication, but also, independently, because (without ever having said it) he wished his work to have the scale of his religious preoccupations...

He never said it, it was you made him say it, you gang of philosophical *curés*, of blind cops, of literate warrant-officers. What, after all, did Kafka do to you? You never understood a thing about him, you couldn't understand a thing about him, there's no place, fortunately, in your world where there's any risk of my running into you. But was it necessary for you to force the sombre wonders of Kafka's world, which communicates through broad subterranean channels with that of Roussel, with that of Lewis Carroll, to fit the hatter's block of your stupidity? Why, oh why, haven't you exercised your interpretative talents on Bernanos, or Germaine Beaumont, who offer so many opportunities? Admit it, it's something to cry over when one sees a certain Monsieur Carrive penning the following pretty thoughts in his introduction to a rather bad translation of *The Great Wall of China*:

The fragments that remain to us reveal one of the forms of the question with which, in a particularly intense way, Kafka's thought finds itself engaged: *Man at grips with the Transcendent, that is to say, in the Nietzschean period of "the death of God,"* with negativity, *in some measure the Transcendent. For, with Kafka, God remains unnamed and does not appear (or barely at all, as here, in obscure allegories).*

Ah yes, you may well say it, Monsieur Carrive, that he remains unnamed, your God. But you really should explain to us why, when he is made man and comes down into the castle, it is to write to the girls of the village, to the very best of appearances, proposing to bugger them. It is a terrible pity that Kafka should be dead, for he could not often (what! with Max Brod always at

REPUBLIQUE FRANÇAISE

Liberty — Egalité — Fraternité

Year_____   No._____

LICENCE TO LIVE VALID FOR ONE YEAR

Prefect of the département of _____

In view of the decree of 23 May 1946 bearing upon rules regarding the existence of individuals subject to our control and especially its Article 9;

In view of the favourable opinion of the departments of health, censuses and police;

Granted on condition of the strict observance of the instructions listed overleaf, this document licences M. ....

born the................ at ....

of ....

born the .... at .... *Licence to Live* No. ....

and ....

born the .... at .... *Licence to Live* No. ....

Profession: ....

Nationality: ....

Mode of acquisition of that nationality: birth, marriage, naturalisation (delete where inapplicable)

Family situation: unmarried, married, widowed, divorced (delete where inapplicable).

Licence to Live No. of spouse (if applicable) ....

Licence to Live Nos. of children (if applicable) ....

Place of residence at time of granting of Licence: ....

Valid for the territory of: ....

Medical certificate no:......... Identity-card no: .... Elector's card no: .... Ration-card no:............

Social Assurance Reference no:............. Military Status:...

DESCRIPTION

Height: .... Weight: .... Nose: Bridge...................... Base.........................

Hair: ....   Length: ....

Moustache: ....   Blood group: ....

Eyes: ....   Cephalic index: ....

Colour: ....   Overall shape of face: ....

Distinguishing features: ....

FINGERPRINT: SIGNATURE OF PERMIT HOLDER

Affix monthly stamp here   ....

                                          ....the..........................

J F M A M J J A S O N D   Prefect of the département of..............

NOTE

I. The *Licence to Live* is issued for one year only and is not valid unless it bears the control-stamp of the current month. The issue of the Permit does not necessarily mean that it will be validated at the time of the monthly checks, the control Commissions remaining free to make a ruling not subject to appeal if new facts seem to them to justify the withdrawal of the Licence.

II. The bearer must at all times carry the Licence, present it whenever so requested by Agents of the Authority as also to persons sheltering or lodging him, for whatever reason, even free of charge, or who rent him unfurnished premises, these persons being held responsible to check the validity of the said Licence and, subject to the gravest penalties, immediately to report any individual whose papers are not in order.

III. Foreigners in category A are subject to weekly checks. Foreigners in category B, comprising nationals of the following countries: Albania, Bulgaria, Greece, Hungary, Italy, Poland, Romania, as well as American citizens of colour (by virtue of the Franco-American convention of 28 October 1946) and all indigenous nationals of the French Union[53] can obtain only a temporary *Licence to Live*, which they must have stamped daily.

IV. Every person changing domicile or residence, even within the limits of the commune, must *before their departure* have their *Licence to Live* countersigned by the Commissaire de Police (failing that by the Maire) specifying very precisely the place to which they must go and *stating exactly the reasons leading them to effect the change.* Movements, even temporary, beyond the limits of the habitual *département* of residence will be authorised only after the interested party has obtained a *Licence to Live* in each of the *départements* through which they will have to travel to reach their destination. All persons who find themselves, even in transit, within the limits of a *département* and who cannot produce a *Licence to Live* granted by that same *département* will be considered as being without any *Licence to Live.*

V. Parents are invited to provide their children *at birth* with a valid *Licence to Live.* No infant aged more than one week can escape the sanctions provided for by law if found without a personal *Licence to Live*, the parents' *Licence to Live* in no case being valid in its place.

VI. Any person who for reasons of health has been unable to go and have their *Licence to Live* stamped is obliged to provide themselves with a medical certificate countersigned by the Commissaire de Police (failing that by the Maire). Interested parties are warned that domiciliary checks will be carried out at any hour of the day or night by Agents of the Authority.

VII. Every French citizen not in possession of a *Licence to Live* or whose *Licence to Live* is not in order will be liable to capital punishment, to be carried out immediately at the expense of the interested party, without prejudice to the other penalties provided for in article 486, section 12 of the Penal Code. Foreign citizens will in addition be subject to deportation.

Facsimile of *Licence to Live* (left: recto, above: verso), see **Emancipation**.

his side!) have had a laugh, but how he'd have split his sides reading this:

We are well aware of the impermeability *of the Chinese mind to Revelation and to all theology, its realism of the Essential, simultaneous moreover, with its* formalism. *So many reasons for the present affabulation... By virtue of its antiquity China is contiguous with the very sources of Time, and, by reason of its immensity, it commingles with Space. The Transcendent (the Emperor and Peking) would appear to be blended into these two Infinities.*

Monsieur Carrive, an honorary Chinese, is capable, moreover, of surpassing himself. I'm not making any of this up:

(Hence, as regards the Emperor and the Laws of the "Council of Chiefs," and the revolutionary nihilism of, notably, the younger generations, these near-biblical metaphors, these remarks through which there passes, as it were, a breath of Joseph de Maistre!)

Joseph de Maistre! Kafka!! Together!!![54]

One could laugh, or weep, or go and murder Monsieur Carrive. However, seeing that Monsieur Carrive keeps company with Joseph de Maistre, one might rather hope that an exhalation of Joseph de Maistre — a fart probably — might come and asphyxiate Monsieur Carrive before he has time to breed. Pending the accomplishment of that happy cleansing, we do him the kindness of appending the name of the ingenious Monsieur H.-J. Schoeps. Note 6 of the said preface, p. 14:

6. See in Metamorphosis, Gallimard edition, the story The Cares of a Family Man. *As H.-J. Schoeps has pointed out, the* Family Man *here is God.*

Well, there you are then, the Family Man is God — Monsieur Schoeps as well, Odradek of course, and consequently the late Monsieur Carrive!

Our courage fails us when it comes to handling such filth. I have them here before me, on the table, stuck to Kafka like crab-lice to a lovely head of hair. He's mine, is Kafka... no, mine... if you don't mind... after you... don't push,

there's enough for everybody, even the Christian Scientists... and suppose I explain to you, suppose I unearth the formal contents...

For the best texts on Kafka one should perhaps peruse Mademoiselle Marthe Robert's *Introduction à la lecture de Kafka.* My sense of propriety, that old-world gallantry that is peculiar to myself, the fear of distressing her or suffering her disdain restrain me from proclaiming all the good opinions I have of her eminently conciliatory work. I can only set it beside that eminently useful tome which contains an introduction in French prose to the poems of Mallarmé. Thank you, Madame Marthe, there are tasks one owes to humanity. Thank you for explaining to us — it's so pleasant when teacher speaks nicely to her pupils — that:

"In Our Synagogue" represents in Kafka's work a veritable legend of amnesia.

that:

La Bête à la face monstreuse... c'est la grande pensée oubliée que l'homme a rejeté loin de lui. [The beast with the monstrous face... is the great forgotten thought man has cast away far from him.]

Anyhow I think that ought to read *rejetée.*

But tell me, Madame Richard, just what is that stick the sacristan's grandfather takes up to expel the animal, eh? You really ought to have an idea ... don't you think? Ah, this generation no longer reads Freud, that's for sure... But, leaving that aside, nothing escapes her, neither what Monsieur de Poiton means in *L'Invité des Morts,* nor the fact that Kafka

has drawn the argument of the story New Lamps *from his experience as an employee of the insurance company which, in some measure, laid bare to him the other side of the world of work.*

And that's it — work!

It's not funny, what I'm up to at the moment, but it wasn't me that started it. I repeat, Kafka didn't do anything to them, all these tight-arsed pedants who don't understand the usage of the word "dream." All the same, can one — without, when it comes to the crunch, bawling out shit at the top of one's voice — read the prose of a Master Klossowski, faced with the *Diaries*? Where is it they go to find it all? Where do they reckon to have read that in Kafka? But they churn out their texts, those pustular holy-water-font-haunters.[55]

Kafka's Diaries are first and foremost the journal of a sick man in search of healing. Not a sick man who, like Nietzsche, at once lucid and delirious, merges by degrees into his sickness: Kafka does not admit tragedy as a solution. But he desires health for the full expansion of the resources he senses within him... Kafka's work in its entirety breathes the expectation of the messianic Kingdom. For him health, but also the justified enjoyment of health, coincide with the coming of the Kingdom, and since the Kingdom has not yet come for anyone, none can overestimate that which still escapes everyone: health will then be sanctity.

Admit honestly that to find that in Kafka, you must first put it there. But there is no law to prevent the Klossowskis[56] from performing their religious duties[57] where they see fit. And there are fifty-three pages like that, culminating in a brilliantly senile couplet about Don Quixote and Sancho Panza... Anyhow... Gallifet died comfortably in his bed...[58]

The Penal Colony, now translated into Franco-Swiss... But no... I haven't the strength to open the book... there was a moment, too extraordinary, in my personal life... I can't take any more... Kafka the Jew, Kafka the candidate for marriage, for sainthood, Kafka expecting the Messiah, Zarathustra, Kafka the existentialist... cheer up, we're almost there, one last effort... let's dig just once more at random into the heap. Here's a certain François Léger's conclusion to his article *From Job to Kafka* (*Cahiers du Sud*, March-April 1945):

We cannot live, here and now, in the Father's Kingdom: we cannot possess God, any more than we can be totally separated from him. The Son brings separation from God, and at the same time his possession, sin, and at the *same time redemption: anguish, and at the same time eternity. This simultaneity is faith.*

Man can never say he has Faith. Does Christ bring to man anything other than an expectation — Kafka's expectation?

After that it remains only to write an interpretation of Kafka taking as its basis ornithology, or philately — why not? I undertake to demonstrate that *Amerika* (less the two chapters no doubt judged obscene by Max Brod and consequently suppressed for that reason) is the impassioned search for a specimen, in mint condition, without cancellation, of the 1874 two-cents Cape of Good Hope; there's no mistake about it.

Having thoroughly stirred up the dunghill of idealism, I think I can do no better than to hand over the fork to my very dear friend the Reverend Charles Lutwidge Dodgson. Let him once and for all give the answer to the verminous scapulars cited above. I am aware that this haughty retort is well beyond their comprehension, and that the lines that follow are beginning to be well known. But they cannot too frequently be quoted, and it will clear the atmosphere:

I was walking on a hillside, alone, one bright summer day, when suddenly there came into my head one line of verse — one solitary line — "For the Snark was a Boojum, you see." I knew not what it meant, then: I know not what it means, now; but I wrote it down: and, sometime afterwards, the rest of the stanza occurred to me, that being its last line: and so by degrees, at odd moments during the next year or two, the rest of the poem pieced itself together, that being its last stanza. Periodically I have received courteous letters from strangers begging to know whether The Hunting of the Snark is an allegory, or contains some hidden moral, or is a political satire: and for all such questions I have but one answer, "I DON'T KNOW!"[59]

ESENPLUSH or ESENPLOSH (KASPAR VAN), known as THE ELDER. — Painter of historical and

 genre pieces and of portraits, born (probably) at Bewewyk about 1596, died Hoogeven after 1649. The works of this artist are often confused with those of Joost Esenbeck. According to some authors it might even be possible that Esenplush and Esenback never existed and that the paintings that figure under their names in collections and museums might be the work of Johan Osenplick, known as the crocodile of Haarlem. However Mademoiselle Lapompe de Beaugremard, in a learned study she devoted to Esenplush (*Jahrbuch der kunsthistorischen Sammlungen allerh. Kaiserhauses*, Vol XXXVI, 1916) draws attention to the stylistic analogies (curvilinear treatment of loose-ends of draperies, protuberant eyeballs, diagonal jawbones) that link Esenplush with Rafael Sanguineto and concludes that the two painters are in fact one and the same person. To escape religious persecution Esenplush would appear to have fled the Low Countries at a very early age and settled in the outskirts of Mantua. Mademoiselle Lapompe de Beaugremard expressly recognises his style in an altarpiece in the church of San Francesco at Metesila: *Magistrates playing at cards with women flower-sellers in a tavern, surprised by their wives during divine service.* Without entirely falling in with the opinion of Mademoiselle Lapompe de Beaugremard, Professor Jolilooloo and the Abbé Requin are inclined to recognise in Esenplush an artist from the North firmly attached to his iconographic tradition, but none the less having to a certain degree undergone an italo-franco-catalan influence, more discernible however in the geometry of *funnel-pleats* than in the typology of persons represented.

[ESQUIMAU] ESKIMO. — The Eskimo, the sage, is he who quietly awaited the middle of the twentieth century to make the transition from the upper gallery to the first-tier boxes. Tomorrow the Grands Boulevards, via Fort Yukon, six months under acetylene-lighting, its enormous brothels — "The Great Bear," "Old Jonah's" — where the native beauty, the idol macerated in piss is vainly to be pursued.

Unless... There is no reason positively to despair of seeing born, in conformity with the prophesy, as soon as the earth is exploited beyond the line that joins Nounivak and Farewell, a *corona borealis*, that is to say an immense aurora borealis no longer merely lighting but providing heat, the first effect of which will be to unleash on the planet, *rut* in all its power. Everywhere the puny human systems will fall apart. One of the affectations of the corona borealis will be to manifest itself and make itself felt first and foremost through the windows of the meeting-place of the Leningrad Writers' Committee (cf. Magritte's painting "A Panic in the Middle Ages").[60]

Predestined from the start for the future Phenomenon, the ivory-bespectacled Eskimo in the sempiternal snowstorm, is the sculptor, engraver, poet — who, par excellence, plunges us into "forgetfulness of existing in an epoch that survives beauty." We know little — what does one ever know? — of the meaning, and even the use of the various types of Eskimo masks — admirable above all others, gifted to the highest degree with magnetic power and the vigour to eclipse all other specimens of the art of imagination, from antiquity to our times. At most it has been tentatively suggested that many of their masks, devoid of religious intent, have been conceived in such a way as to provoke a reaction on the borderlands of laughter and fear and have been the object of tournaments of black humour between villages. Europeans, recently affected by a harsh winter, might do well to make this their own perspective, to establish a precise discrimination between that which, seen from that viewpoint, might not last and might last.

Might not last:	Might last:
. . . .	*Joyeux farceurs,* Henri
. . . .	Rousseau; the Obelisk;
. . . .	the Moebius strip; Alfr-
. . . .	red Jarry's *La Dragonne;*
. . . .	Avagadro's number;[61]
. . . .	the ai (or three-toed
. . . .	sloth); Benjamin Péret's
. . . .	*Main forte;* Marcel Du-
. . . .	champ's *griffe volante,* &c.

ESSENCE. — Extremely volatile substance extracted from books of piety and philosophy. According to certain recent authors essence does not exist, it is born. It is also said that it essencifies itself since it has no cessation whose senses it has not subjected to census. This, one senses, does not happen without accessory offence to that innocent who imagines one assays it in censing knowledge.

[ESSOR] SOARING FLIGHT. — Before undertaking an aerial voyage with the aim of observing a radiant point, it is as well to assure oneself, by the resolution of a horary triangle, that that point in the celestial canopy possesses, at the time of its greatest elevation above the horizon, a sufficient zenith-distance. If this is not so, it will be necessary for the astronomical balloon to be launched from a station closer to the equator for the ascent to be carried out successfully.

Two precautions are necessary. The first is to provide the aerostat with a small portable electric lamp of at most a fifth of a candlepower to light the draughtsman who traces the trajectories without depriving his eye of the exquisite sensitivity it acquires in the darkness. The second is to lessen, as far as possible, what we might call the angle of the balloon, that is to say the amplitude of the small circle situated about the zenith and which occupies a part of the celestial sphere. By giving astronomical balloons the shape of a pear, by lengthening the suspension-cables in a suitable manner, Monsieur Besançon believes he could construct astronomical balloons in which the angles would not reach twenty degrees.

The success of the experiment of 14 November was complete. Although the heavens had been observed from a large number of stations, the radiant point was not seen except aboard the balloon "Alliance." Disappointment was general along a band obliquely crossing the entire surface of the earth. In Paris the fog was unusually opaque, but it was only 200 metres in depth. Arriving, in effect, in the zone where the sky was admirably clear, the three aerial travellers occupying the nacelle of the "Alliance" noted with astonishment how the church of the Sacré Cœur and the Eiffel Tower pierced the sea of clouds like two standing pricks.

[ESTAFETTE] DISPATCH-RIDER. — The bicycle will be employed not only for the dispatch-rider service, but also to allow detachments of infantry to manoeuvre with the cavalry and augment its lethal effectiveness. Germany, in its turn, envisages using the new means of locomotion for the transport of artillery and munitions.

One of the most ingenious armaments-plants of our epoch, the Maxim's Company, has just carried out in England a very interesting trial: it has manufactured a tricycle-cannon. This is a tandem-tricycle, activated by two artillerymen, the hind-carriage of which carries two Maxim guns along with their mountings and ammunition. The weight of the whole vehicle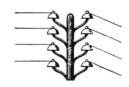

is in the region of 150 kilos. The prospect of hauling such a weight would cause many a cyclist to pull a wry face. But, once a satisfactory mechanism has been adapted for the system, they will have a piece of equipment able to render considerable services and, at all events, capable in cases of urgency, of advancing along roads at a lightning speed not to be expected of horses. For firing, the piece is placed on a mounting shaped like a tripod, which can be folded for transportation. A single gunner suffices to operate it. He is seated on a saddle fixed to the rear leg of the tripod. This somewhat resembles the arquebus of former times and its support.

One of the most remarkable peculiarities of the Maxim gun is that, the first shot fired, fire can continue uninterrupted and automatically, the gunner having as his sole preoccupation only to keep his finger constantly pressed to the trigger, and to aim the weapon.

An ingenious mechanism utilises, in effect, the force of the recoil to open the breech, to extract the case of the spent cartridge, introduce a new one, and fire.

To prevent overheating, the barrel of the gun is encased in a water-filled cooling-jacket.

[ESTHETIQUE] AESTHETIC(S). — Has inherited, although nobody has quite realised this, along with the prerogatives of religion and morality, even those of political sovereignty. Naturally, in proportion to these new obligations, aesthetic activity as it is currently practised, is untenable: the attitude of art for art's sake because in actuality it is the abandonment of obligations; the attitude of engagement because it in fact subordinates the life of the emotions — which can have no end but the life of the emotions — to some utilitarian activity. But no attention is paid to this truth: "there is nothing superior to intensity of emotion," since it is confused with a vitiated taste, rather than seized as an exigency.

[ESTIME, NAVIGATION À LA] NAVIGATION BY DEAD RECKONING . — The first mate came on to the bridge, to my great surprise, as it wasn't time for his watch and I hadn't been expecting him. He drew me aside against the handrail, and I could  see by his dishevelled hair and his puffy eyes that he had just woken up. I asked him why he had left his bunk in the middle of his sleep and he said, "Excuse me, captain, I wasn't asleep, I haven't closed an eye for a fortnight. I'd like to talk to you, but not here."
The steersman was in the way, I told the first lieutenant to fetch me from my cabin if I was needed, and the mate and I went down below. I don't like people to go sleepless for a fortnight on board the "Valdivia," especially if they have responsible jobs.

My first mate is a very tall, very thin man with a dense black beard. Imagine my surprise when instead of speaking he burst into tears. A man who never touches drink! He wept copiously, to my great embarrassment, and when he suddenly flung himself on the ground at my feet, I didn't know what to do with myself. He was an old friend of mine and I tried to make him stand up. I might have lost my temper, I'd have been quite justified, but we'd been in love with the same woman twenty years earlier and he'd not been quite so lucky as I had. What an awkward fix for the captain of a passenger-carrying cargo-boat! But I behaved with great propriety. I went back to sit in my armchair as if I were tacitly giving him permission to kneel there weeping as long as he liked. At last he got up, and again he came towards me with his eyes downcast and took me by the hand and said: "Captain, I've been deceiving you, the fourth hold is full of Chinamen." I stared at him, gaping, and he began to talk very fast, like a man at the end of his tether chucking down sacks of cement.

That's what life is like, though. For forty years you're respected by all the ship-owners and then, suddenly, you find yourself transporting Chinamen without knowing it.

"Yes, yes, it's true, Captain, but it's not my fault, I swear it isn't. My only mistake — and it's a shocking one, I admit — was not to have told you earlier. The cold-storage engineer did it all, together with the ship-chandler from Banjoevanjie. That's why Mexican piastres were flying about when we called at Mormigao, and why it took two men each to bring those two on board again. There's no end to their tricks. And now the fourth hold is full of Chinamen, live ones, dead ones in coffins, empty coffins for the live ones when they die, and the stink's dreadful. And all the Patna rice we had so much difficulty in stowing, they've chucked it all away. At least I suppose so, I didn't see them at it, but they must have put the cargo somewhere to make room for their Chinamen. It must have happened a couple of nights before we arrived, I saw nothing and heard nothing, but neither did you, Captain, which only goes to show how quietly they must have set about it. And I didn't see the Chinamen embarking either, but they're on board none the less. It began soon after Mormigao. I heard them on the other side of the wall, my cabin's so close to the fourth hold — by the way, Captain, it's hardly the sort of cabin for a first mate, but then it's not for me to say so. At first I thought it was rats, they were rustling about all night, dragging along sacks of dead leaves, but on the third night I knew by the smell that came through a crack in the wall that they were Chinamen — yellow rats. For the last fortnight, whenever I've not been on the bridge I've stayed with my ear glued to the wall, listening. And now I wonder how I could have been so long without guessing. But what could I have done all on my own? And if I'd told you it would have been still worse, for you'd have had the hold broken open immediately and if those Chinese hadn't been there I'd have been taken for a loony, a dangerous loony not fit to be first mate on the "Valdivia." And yet they are there, I can hear them the whole time, even from here — they're whispering away as fast as they can in Chinese. They're so cunning! Nobody on board knows about them, except the cold-storage engineer of course, and he'll deny everything, but they're there, Captain, they've fixed up everything in the hold in their own way, they've even got a little temple with sticks burning in front of it, a real horror. And what are they thinking about, what are they planning in there, in the dark? Why was I so afraid of making a fool of myself, Captain, why didn't I dare tell you earlier? Now do what you like, I don't care about anything, I'm going to be able to go to sleep and they can burst their lungs yelling the other side of the wall, I shan't wake up in a hurry."

And that was that! He'd got it off his chest, and he went to sleep; he's been asleep for three days now, with the tear-marks still on his cheeks and on his beard. But I walk up and down on the bridge, and I can't rest, and I daren't look towards the stern of the "Valdivia." I've had the corners of the tarpaulins lined, and nobody understands why. I can't stand the sight of a Chinaman and maybe there are three hundred of them in there. We shall find out when we arrive, or rather, if I can help it, we shan't. I shall shut my eyes, the cold-storage engineer will take off his Chinamen quietly and nobody will be any the wiser. For the first mate's crazy, two men all by themselves could never have emptied a hold without being noticed. The rice must still be there, for sure, they can't have eaten it all. In the dead middle of the night, when nobody can see me, I lay my ear against the wall, but I can't hear anything at all. Perhaps there are no Chinese in the hold. After all the first mate never saw them, but then he manages to hear such a lot of things... And I've got nobody to complain to, it's all very sad and depressing. I shall feel easier in my mind when we've left Vancouver, and later on, much later on, I'll have the hold opened up. But Vancouver is still a long way off, the winds are against us, we're burning too much coal, the woman passenger in cabin six

is eight months pregnant and we knew nothing about it, and now I've got to find somebody to take the first mate's watch. It's a terrible lot of worry for one man to bear.

[ESTORGISSEMENT] ESTORGISATION. — We apologise for being unable to provide any definitive clarification of this term, the importance of which nevertheless is perfectly obvious. Is it, as Monsieur Merleau-Ponty, following Husserl, would have it, an *Abschattung*, the clarification of which about 1970 would initiate a long series of perceptive troubles and cognitive disturbances? But Monsieur Jean Wahl, in a celebrated sonnet, rises up, with good reason, against this with the least premature assertion and relates *estorgissement* to *Auseinandersetzung*, a neologism employed by Heidegger, made up of the words *aus* (Lat. *ex*), *einander* (together, mutually) and *Setzung* (the act of placing). For his part, Monsieur Gabriel Marcel establishes a similar comparison when he links the *moi orant* with the *orant étant*. Nevertheless, as Monsieur Jean-Paul Sartre writes: "that which links the anterior with the posterior is precisely nothing" (*L'Être et le Néant*, p. 64), and he aptly adds: "The ontico-ontological parallelism of the conatus

bases its otherness on an eristic incompletion with regard to the known-knowing-known." Whence, act.

[ETAT] STATE. — The concept of the state has arisen, like many others, from the tendentious association of two words. People have chosen to confuse state, manner of being, with state, central power, and this latter term has by degrees acquired the ineluctable character of a natural necessity, which initially in no way existed. It is thus that the state, government, became *de facto* the state, and *état civil*, civil status, a state of mind. Now, if men's immemorial experience of the state, administration, reduces them to a state, a situation, less and less bearable, it is revealing to note that, on the other hand, the few examples of non-state, absence of government, coincide with a state, a disposition of total cheerfulness among individuals. The desolate tundra that echoes to the laughter of the Eskimos is an impressive example. It is plain that the non-state is the only state that can henceforth be tolerated.

[ETATS-UNIS] UNITED STATES. — *Etym.* In the cosmology of the Indians of Arizona to the right of ecstasy, between ether and *étui* [case, box, holster], is found *etase*. In every generation the Macaw clan bestows upon one of its members the sacred name of "Medicine-Flower" or *Etase Zuni*.

ET CETERA. — That which parents do not wish to tell children.

[ETENDARD] STANDARD. — Literature has always been honoured in France. Anatole was a man of letters. In his posthumous work, *Souvenirs d'un existence triste*, which was interrupted by the premature death of the author, we find the following thoughts which throw a searching light on the sentiments Anatole held dear regarding his vocation:

"The soldier defends his country against foreigners; the constable, against its citizens. The priest points out to the reverential people the altars where the Lord is enthroned. No state merits the name that is not sustained by the conjoined efforts of priest, constable and soldier. From this it follows that the poet, who incarnates them in one person, is the veritable Prince of the state. As priest he fills the chasm between the various classes of society with a sublime song that exalts the secret fraternity of all Frenchmen; as a soldier he defends our language against neologisms; as a constable he defends it against those wretches who dare take those liberties with it which, whilst not subject to the rigours of the law, are none the less prejudicial to gallic decency, which is, as everybody knows, the most subtle of our qualities." (See **Erudition** and **Euphorie**.)

[ETERNITE] ETERNITY. — Eternity appears to me in the form of an ether which is immobile and, as a consequence, is not luminous. Luminous ether I shall call *circular mobile* and perishable. And I deduce from Aristotle (*On the Heavens*) that it is becoming to write *ethernity*.

[ETHIQUE] ETHICS. — An explorer returning from a long stay among the Jivaro Indians of the Amazon, those great head-hunters universally famed for their art of shrinking them — which lends a new dimension to the "to be or not to be" of our ancestors — told us that of all the objects he had been in a position to present to them, there was none that had exercised a greater fascination over them and that seemingly provoked a more lively desire for possession than pins. Being away for a day, he had been curious enough to leave a great many of these lying about in plain view in his shelter (not without having duly counted them), and in such a way that many of the interested parties discovered them. On his return he was able to ascertain that visits had been incessant: yet not a single pin was missing (an incentive for an edifying ethnology).

[ETOILE] STAR.[62] — Roland de Mendebourg was born into a noble family in the Bourbonnais, a province where, at that period, following a singular custom, every infant of distinction was placed at birth in the hands of an astrologer who, seeking out the star that presided over its coming into the world, employed a procedure peculiar to the individual in inscribing their name onto the nape of their neck in the form of a monogram. Employing a wary delicacy, with improvised instruments, the man of science would, one by one, introduce minuscule needles, prodigiously fine, barely a *ligne* in length and magnetised at the point, into the skin at the back of the neck and perpendicular thereto, so arranging them that, at the end of the operation, their clustered mass, visible below the epidermis, constituted the desired figure, thenceforth forever fixed. The aim of the operation was to place the subject, for their entire life, in contact with the appointed star which, by means of its magnetic effluvia, attracted by the magnetised points, would protect and guide them.

The nape of the neck was chosen because, in the great majority of cases, the effluvia, falling from the heavens, would have to pass through the brain before reaching the needles, and thus shed precious light in the seat of thought.

[EUCLIDE] EUCLID. — Must be held responsible for a lengthy machination of subtle virulence.

This glorious geometrician, whose peaceable temperament history ironically reports, did not recoil before any effort to compel men to recognise the truth of polyhedra. With a perfectly lucid and patient malice, disdaining to be a secret stockbreeder, it is the mind of man that he has sought to deliver over as nourishment for polyhedra. In "truth" it is the sole nourishment that suits them.

The mind is the place where metamorphoses are metamorphosed: an enterprise such as his could not ignore this. The diabolical craftiness of this Greek is to have, in full awareness, tossed into it the ravaging double infinity of right-angled triangles.

To achieve his ends, he knew moreover, how to find the restricted form of communication he needed. A logical and deductive form whereby the mind bewitches itself, as if in a set of mirrors which Euclid was the first to make axiomatically parallel.

He therefore wrote twelve books of geometry, none of which treat of polyhedra, but each of which bears witness to his brilliant culpability.

Legend has it that Euphorbus, "the well-nourished," was the first Greek to have traced out some shadows of geometrical "Ideas" on the sands of Ionian beaches. It is probable that he traced out interesting and complicated figures there.

The considerable ambition of Euclid, some centuries later, was to demonstrate the meanest and simplest of figures. The clear labyrinth of Euclid does not unveil the richer design of Euphorbus before the 47th and last proposition of Book 2.

Euclid's audacity, in effect, is to have demanded that we grant as true only properties so evident and humble that nobody other than he would have dared to mention them. This pedant entreats us, to cite an example familiar to all, that we permit him to draw a straight line between two distinct points. Who would have had the impudence to refuse him that request without being thereby removed from the company of geometricians?

Poetically unveiling his method, Euclid finally dares to name these primitive elements of the emerging fascination.

Axioms and Postulates. The absence of any secret and transparency of procedure are the essential conditions of his tenebrous artifices.

Beginning with a few axioms, the twelve books of geometry construct, by rigorous logical deduction, a considerable edifice of superimposed levels: the very tree of science. The base is at once so frail and so solid that it seems like the dream of a dream, reposing wholly upon itself.

If the mind then, well before the 13th book, is irremediably delivered over to polyhedra, that is because they endlessly contain their own and identical supercession, their own and identical destruction.

To demand with such insistence of pupils that they concede to the master as true a small number of propositions which he does not demonstrate is to incite them either to demonstrate them for themselves, or else, if that is not realisable, not to concede them to him. It is to invite them to construct other geometrical edifices in which certain axioms would be changed into signs; they would thereby have to call the staircases of the temple columns, and transform the statue of the god into the door.

In the domain of the mind, so obvious is the attitude they imply, that words of scandal, of disrespect and insolence are emptied of meaning and realistic usage.

To turn Euclid's thought against itself allows one to understand it properly. It is to perceive that only a single necessary condition is sufficient to support the whole geometrical construction: it must not contain a contradiction that would cause it to collapse upon itself. Apart from that, everything is permissible. Euclid's true pupils are the architects of non-Euclidean geometries.

What makes Euclid's endeavour so propitious is having finally led geometry and, by its example all mathematics, to become a game in all ways comparable to chess, if, that is, chess had an infinity of pieces and, as a consequence, did not exist. The pieces in the geometrical game are not, it is true, diverse — points, lines and planes; on the other hand, they are not finite in number.

What makes Euclid's endeavour so infernal has finally led to the present situation: the player is a finite being who knows and wishes himself finite, he can manipulate only a finite number of objects with certainty, pronounce reasonably only a finite number of words; but, seated at the geometric chessboard, which he would have infinite, he nevertheless insists upon playing and winning all the games possible by methods entirely transparent and finite.

Which plainly shows that he must construct his infinite chessboard at the same time as he teaches himself to play correctly. He does not accept that the game should at any moment be "given" to him.

Striving towards that transcendence he wishes simultaneously to reduce and create, only one method offers itself to the player's pride: the axiomatic formalism whose origin is precisely the basis of Euclid's constructive thought. It consists, in its modern form, of the manipulation of a finite number of symbols, that is to say recognisable signs written on paper, with the aid of a finite number of rules of the game. These symbols replace without ambiguity the infinity of pieces and possible moves. It is curious and meaningful that this first part of the method should be readily practicable and fruitful.

The infinite reappears in so far as the signs can

be manipulated in an infinity of ways. This infinity cannot be suppressed, but it is not an obstacle to the finite conduct of the game. The unique and inevitable requirement is to be able to play each determined game without in any of them encountering a wall reflecting its own derision. The sole obstacle, in effect, would be to find realisable in the theory two contradictory propositions.

The logical rules that make up part of the game have as a consequence that, of two contradictory propositions, it results that both propositions are true and both are false. Which means, roughly speaking, that one could play without knowing the rules of the game, which would be devoid of interest.

Thus, for such a game to "exist," it should be shown that such a catastrophe will never take place, and it is indispensable to show this.

The signs and the rules of the game constitute very exactly a language which makes the geometrical universe a discourse. The study of the different correct sentences of this language, a translation of the realisable games, form its syntax. The problem to be solved, of non-contradiction, is thus posed in a discourse which speaks of the syntax and not at the level of the language. To get the better of this problem, it is necessary in its turn to transform the syntax, which is infinite, into a finite number of signs and rules of the game, thus to formalise that syntax into a finite and manageable "metalanguage." But the problem of non-contradiction again poses itself for the metalanguage, as it did for the initial language. It must be treated in the same way. We then see metalanguages and the metasciences they define indefinitely superimposed. This new Tower of Babel introduces into the transparency of the mind an infinity and a confusion from which there is no escape.

Until 1929 the majority of axiomaticians believed however in the possibility of a radical finitude.

It was hoped that the metalanguages might be amenable to being translated into a unique and simple language.

And then a theorem of mathematical logic came upon the scene to scupper the hopes of those who had not appreciated Euclid's true greatness.[63]

This theorem is the result of efforts undertaken to find what, in the syntax of a language, was expressible in the lower formalism of the language.

Now it seems proven, inversely, that any metalanguage is infinitely richer than, and as irreducible, as the initial language.

This is decisive: the mind cannot seek to close itself in upon itself without being swept away in a vertiginous destruction.

The rigorous desire for an absolute transparency is transformed into an abandonment to the night.

If the truth of polyhedra is to be a game of signs devoid of meanings other than those deriving from the structure of the rules of the game, then the demonstrable absence of a proof of non-contradiction no longer leaves the geometrical dream based upon the dream of that dream. The truth of polyhedra coincides with the infinite liberty of a player whose finitude is at that point so insurmountable that only the demonstration of that finitude escapes him. The failure should be interpreted as both the condition and the meaning of the game.

It is to believe in God to think of Lautréamont that he might have been the first to deposit a time-bomb in the human mind, and it is timorous to wish to limit its destructive power, to isolate him so strangely. The eulogies to mathematics contained in *Les Chants de Maldoror* are not alien to the work.

Is it not encouraging to recognise that the structure of the mind is such that any device placed in it — be it even a pure mathematical crystal — should finally reveal itself, for the mind, as a liberating time-bomb?

[EUPHORIE] EUPHORIA. — It surely suffices to glance over the fragment earlier to be persuaded that Anatole de Fondpierre had in mind nothing less than to ride roughshod over the fine traditions of his family. What is more, it must be remarked that he drew no attention to himself until such time as he began to lose his hair. I am particularly anxious to stress this point as proof that the falling out of his hair was the cause of his moral downfall. A poet of some standing, a fierce and respected democrat, Monsieur Anatole de Fondpierre incurred the blame of no party while his hair remained magnificent, wavy and sweet-scented. His concierge regarded him as a god, not without reason, since he never deigned to greet her.

Deflowered at thirteen, and in that at one with all the boys of the village, by Madame Pilou, the cattleman's wife, he entered the literary life of Paris the hard way; thanks to the good offices of the famous dramatist Jean Cocteau he was soon famous in his turn and his poems, the saturnism of which was praised by specialists, were published in all the reviews. Soon married, he was quickly divorced from his wife, who had the bad taste to love him; Anatole, modern to the tip of his sex, candidly regarded love as an abomination and held that that sentiment was prejudicial to pleasure. After his divorce, his life was spent between the fashionable bistros and publishers' offices.

In this way he spent ten years, as much at his ease as he pleased; and when, by chance, he found himself short of money, the articles he devoted to the praise of some boxer or other among his acquaintances would free him on the spot from any thought for the morrow. (See **Etendard** and **Examination**.)

[EVAGINATION] EVAGINATION. — The eyes are cortical evaginations.

Human acts are desires, intentions to have

sexual relations, more or less hasty, with living creatures and objects.

All women have hundreds of sexual relations with women and men in the course of the day.

All men...

What man has had the idea of having the sexual character of his skin, of his voice (speaking like a eunuch), of his eyes, removed while speaking to anybody, while looking at a man or a woman?

What woman has had the idea...

[EVALUATION] EVALUATION. — Estimation of the value, price or number of things. Contrary to all stable and regular currencies, it is difficult to estimate the exact value of Evaluation. Nowadays, stability renders evaluation superfluous. Efforts made at contriving to regularise the fluctuations of values have remained fruitless.

So many countries, so many customs.

The evaluation of the price of agricultural products varies along with the destruction of these same products when their abundance threatens to be prejudicial to world markets. Agricultural workers have a different measure to fix the price of wheat from that of major producers. (Major producer = great landowner, grain-merchant or speculator on the cereals market.) These latter have at their disposal an ultra-modern organisation. As soon as a convoy on the high seas has succeeded in jettisoning its cargo of wheat, mixed beforehand with tar, the fact is signalled by radio to the Chicago Stock Exchange and the price of wheat immediately rises by a point. The appreciation thus created is scarcely in keeping with the effort expended. One should, in fact, take into account the difficulties to be surmounted in preventing the sharks from consuming that wheat, which would bring about not only a fall in the market for wheat, but also that for fish.

Evaluation, already difficult as regards secondary products such as wheat or fish, becomes excessively problematical when it concerns creation's crowning achievement — Man.

The most contentious evaluation of all is that of man in his component parts. This results from the disproportion between supply and demand. In the event, the component parts come from workers injured in industrial accidents.

Nothing is more edifying than a study of the Social Assurance catalogue regarding the price of man in his component parts. Every part of the body is evaluated in figures. An amputated leg is equivalent to a bicycle with a spare inner-tube. The loss of two legs is worth a 250cc. motor-cycle equipped with a rear-view mirror and regulation lights. The left arm is evidently not as valuable as the right. The sum obtained for the loss of the right eye falls far short of the price of an up-to-date microscope. On the other hand, for the loss of two eyes one could acquire a self-adjusting chromium-plated microscope. All things included, arms, legs, eyes, lungs, kidneys etc., we arrive at the price of a portable crematorium.

Detailed study of these prices highlights a serious underestimation of a human cadaver in relation to the prices of scrap-metals, which realise more than fifty per cent of their newly manufactured price. Why, then, is it that the remains of a man, who was living until he died, are not worth the price of a few kilos of lime?

[EVANGELIQUE] EVANGELICAL. — Said of a religion which still passes in certain quarters as achieving an advance over Catholicism. In fact the notion it opposes to totalitarian paternalism is that of a mankind free but irremediably damned. The instinct of revolt is thus canalised towards socially inoffensive ends. This is the same notion that we find laicised in Heidegger, a disciple of the Protestant theologians Kierkegaard and Karl Barth.

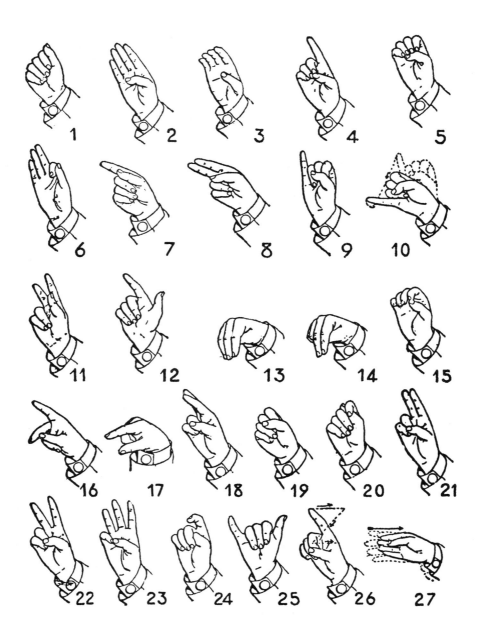

[EROTISME] EROTISM. — 1. Accost. 2. Burgle. 3. Cunnilinguate. 4. Deflower. 5. Ensnare. 6. Fuck. 7. Gallivant. 8. Harass. 9. Irrumate. 10. Jismify. 11. Kink. 12. Lesbianise. 13. Masturbate. 14. Nidify. 15. Occult. 16. Pedicate. 17. Quench. 18. Ream. 19. Syphilise. 20. Tup. 21. Urticate. 22. Violate. 23. Waggle. 24. Xiphoidify. 25. Yonirise. 26. Zoogonise. 27. Recommence.

[EVENTAIL] FAN. — Shell of the pecten genus, the Venus's comb, called in the trade the memnonites' Fan.

EVIDENCE. — Collection of appearances necessary to maintain the world as it is. When it is a serious matter, the word "truth" tends to be employed. Philosophers, however, say "to be." The essential thing is to persuade consciousness that it finds itself before an absolute that cannot be transgressed, and it must be recognised that consciousness — so called ironically since its role consists precisely in having no more consciousness than one wishes it to have — is only too willing thus to persuade itself. It never completely forgets its previous role as a servant, nor the respect owed its former masters, and it uses its freedom as a sort of day off work and strolls stupidly around gazing into the empty shop windows of what is self-evident.

[EXAGERATION] EXAGGERATION. — Nothing is exaggerated.

[EXAMEN] EXAMINATION. — At length came the fatal day when Anatole became aware of the baldness that was threatening him: in *Souvenirs d'une existence triste*, from which the passage quoted above was taken, the most dramatic of all moments is the subject of an extremely beautiful page, one so beautiful that I cannot deny myself the pleasure of copying it; for all that, you will surely be delighted to read it. The pen to which we owe this testament was assuredly qualified to convey every nuance of despair, an account at second hand aims vainly for exactitude and it is not to be compared with the original.

"That morning was very overcast; an uncertain light reigned over the city and the proud and gloomy brows of the women selling violets, so majestic under the carmine-bordered shawl of fine days, were barely visible in the fog... Absent above all was the ray of sunlight which, not long ago, had gilded the portrait of General de Gaulle pasted to the mirror above my washbasin. When I awoke, it seemed to me a grave voice was whispering in my ear this sibylline word: Endives, endives...

"I slowly slipped my feet into my slippers, donned my dressing-gown and, between two sighs, rolled my first cigarette. I always smoke on an empty stomach so as not to have time to delude myself regarding life — this is a habit I formed in my adolescence when I feared I might not know that bitterness which is the condition of all deep thought: unfortunately a practical joker had mixed a small quantity of gunpowder into my tobacco, with the result that I had scarcely lit it when it exploded in my mouth. Such is the ill-nature of men.

"Resolved to bear up against misfortune, I rolled myself a second cigarette and waited, my forehead pressed to the windowpane, for my coffee to boil; a doubt was sowing disorder in my thoughts: I was not certain whether I should brush my teeth. I feared, rightly, the bitterness would be dissipated, hard-won though it was, to which allusion has just been made: and it was essential to the poem I was conceiving. On the other hand, I doubted it was wise to demand too much of the reader. It is one thing to demand of him complete attention, another, inadmissible to tell the truth, to ask him to read you dirty-toothed.

"Thus it was hesitantly that I approached the washbasin, and with a trembling hand that I seized the tube of toothpaste that slept, bloated with mediocre perfumes, on the marble slab, quietly shaded by the silvery necks of the taps.

"The noble countenance of General de Gaulle attracted my gaze; I wished to address him a sort of morning prayer; but at that precise moment I know not what demon caused my eyes to settle on the mirror itself, in which my image was painted... How to express, otherwise than with three suspension-points, my stupefaction? What words are capable of conveying my horror, my despair? I stood there, open-mouthed in dismay at my image, suspended between my distress and a hideous incredulous laugh that was forcibly wrinkling my lips. I was bald.

"I shall not dwell upon the turmoil into which the discovery I had just made threw me. In the face of such a disaster one can but stay silent. Intense as might be the pain the recollection of that most melancholy of moments causes me, do not think ill of me if I keep it a secret, one which must not on any pretext be divulged: there are things which are not spoken of.

"After several minutes of stupor, during which I contemplated my misfortune in the mirror, I became aware of a subtle change that was taking place in the skies. The rain was no longer falling and the sun was showing its ruddy face through the clouds. My heart began once more to beat: like fish issued from the depths of the southern seas, words were rising to the surface of my memory, prestigious and sonorous words. At the moment when despair was dashing down my thought, a miracle! Poetry was saving me. Overjoyed, I fell upon my pen and, in all haste, wrote a long poem on the vanity of things human, which, embellished with a few thoughts which had occurred to me about the atomic bomb, seemed to me, all things considered, worthy of publication. Such are the blessings of poetry: though they be on the point of perishing, it always offers its chosen-ones something to palliate their sufferings." (See **Euphorie** and **Exempte**.)

[EXCES] EXCESS. — That which goes beyond an ordinary limit, a common measure: *An excess of pleasure makes us wholly languid.* CORNEILLE, *Le Cid*, IV, 5. The excesses to which human beings abandon themselves are regarded with reprobation by the mysterious powers that govern the world: *Who knows indeed, who knows if the angered heavens have been able to tolerate the excess of my happiness.* RACINE, *Iphigénie*, III, 6. Classical good taste condemns excess as an impropriety: *You display a grief that verges upon excess.* CORNEILLE, *Le Cid*, I, 2. Excess is also a source of comic effects: *And always from one excess you throw yourself into the others.* MOLIÈRE, *Tartuffe*, V, 4. With the progress of rationalism, all excess becomes an assault one directs against oneself: *Sanctify your passions as you will, they always punish you with the excesses they cause you to commit.* J.-J. ROUSSEAU, *Lév. d'Ephr.*, 3. By virtue of a similar principle, the excess of only one is a threat to all the rest: *Every excess leads to crime.* VOLTAIRE, *Alzire*, IV, 4. According to the moderns, allowance made for a few romantic effusions, quickly repressed, results in excess, purely and simply from pathology: *Our literature already concerns itself to excess with these matters and recently Jean Schlumberger rightly deplored the place love occupies in it.* ANDRÉ GIDE, *Interviews Imaginaires*, p. 29.

So it is that every state that does not amply make room for daily life and its hurly-burly of deals endlessly concluded, endlessly called in question, falls immediately under a tacitly respected interdict. Lovers are warned that they possess each other without belonging to each other, the body one embraces never being anything other than loaned by the world after the manner of a hired mule which must be returned in good condition, hardly marked at all by the blows with which one has frivolously skimmed its surface. And, just as Michael Kohlhaas[64] does not hesitate, on account of a couple of overworked horses, to unleash a massacre, every contravention of the rules of measured, rhythmical, musical, transcendental and courtly love is punished by the plague, a madness aggravated by frothing at the mouth, amputees'-stumps, decayed teeth, put-out eyes, dementia praecox. A word to the wise.

[EXCITATEUR] EXCITER. — *Phys.* Metal rod terminating in a ball, serving to draw sparks from an electrified body which one wishes to discharge without receiving a shock. The exciter is brought into communication with the natural reservoir and the fluid is transmitted by the intermediary of the instrument. (Baill.)

EXEMPT. — This magnificent text was no doubt written shortly after Monsieur de Fondpierre had lost his hair. How is one not to notice, in passing, that initially he defended himself therefrom by euphoria, and that it is to this strange sentiment that we are indebted for the fine poem to which he alludes, entitled *The Vendôme Column*? — This did not last. — Soon Monsieur de Fondpierre was the prey of the most terrible anguish; which shows that baldness should not afford matter for hilarity and, if it does not seem to deserve to be made a fuss of, it is none the less frequently distressing to its victims. However, this is often the case. Witness Rimbaud who, according to some of the best commentators, became, from the young poet of genius he was at the time of his first flight, that which we know, because, after he quit his paternal roof, nobody any longer mended his shoes.[65]

It only remains for me to tell of the moral downfall of Monsieur de Fondpierre. This was occasioned by his baldness and by that alone. I flatter myself that nobody will dispute this. I further flatter myself that my reader is now persuaded that the only way to forestall other downfalls, similar to this, is that the periwig be restored to favour. However, no digressions: only

the most sober of narratives can do justice to our subject.

As soon as the euphoria had passed, Anatole de Fondpierre found himself face to face with his new misery: an unbearable spectacle, especially to a sensitive soul. After the splendid impertinence of the balmy days, there succeeded a timidity which presaged no good. He no longer showed himself at the café, always offering by way of a reason a cold which excused his being present at fights. However, those of his friends who went in for boxing did not know that he was fobbing them off with empty promises. They found it odd that, from one day to the next he should cease keeping their company, suspecting that in secret their virility was not to his liking, and decided no longer to ask him to write fulsome articles for them. That was by no means his only worry: a police-spy noticed that Anatole was no longer voting, although elections were — as always — important and the big-wigs of all parties had let it be understood that all available votes should be cast in their favour, at the risk of being the cause of France's ruination. Anatole was thenceforth the subject of many a threat: his mail abounded in anonymous letters, thoroughly offensive as regards his person. Finally, to complete the horror, his concierge who, as you are aware, used to venerate him, displayed towards him an inexplicable hostility, all the more intense since she claimed to have long been the victim of his contempt.

Anatole no longer ventured out in the daytime. Shut firmly in his quarters, he spent his time meditating on the wretchedness of his fate. From time to time, in the twilight hours, wrapped in a grey overcoat, a false beard glued to his chin, his eyes gleaming behind the smoky green of his spectacles, he would wander about the city's most melancholy streets. Such was his misery that his literary production suffered grievously: he reached the point of writing only one poem a day. For all that, he was supported by certain persons at the *Trois Obus* who had caught sight of him in one of those questionable cafés which, previously, he had made it a point of honour to ignore. In fact his habit was to haunt obscure corners, barely appearing in public and, when approached, he would utter obscenities. That was not all.

The rest is easily imagined. Anatole was prejudiced against wigs and shared his prejudice with his contemporaries. If he had not chosen to smirk at them, he might have purchased one of those splendid wigs which are, so it is claimed, so well made that even an expert is incapable of detecting them. But Anatole bought a hat. It was then that the difficulty came to light which was in the end to prove insurmountable, and was the reason why Monsieur de Fondpierre, despite his brilliant antecedents, touched the bottom of the cloaca of baseness. The hat on his head, Anatole seemed a young man with a great future; but he had only to remove it to be no more than an elderly nonentity who turned out bad verses.

His whole dignity therefore depended upon his hat; to take it off was to expose himself to the gibes of the first comer, a torment Anatole was above all things anxious to spare himself. It was a matter of finding a way of removing it only in the privacy of his room, so as to be secure from ridicule. Anatole soon joined the anarchist party, which made it possible for him to mock at his ease any flag whatever, and even the French flag; in addition he became a spiritualist and claimed, when a coffin went by, that there was no call for him to uncover for a box in which there was nothing but a handful of ashes; finally he became a pederast and in this way accounted for the lack of politeness he displayed towards women...

And that was the final step. He had reached rock bottom. Anarchist, spiritualist, pederast, he had forgotten all human respect. From this short account I conclude, and I believe the reader will share my opinion, that there is only one way to save these men, too weak to bare their shame in the public gaze, and which for all that is not without its merit, and that is to return the wig to its former favour. (See **Examination** and **Eloge**.)

[EXHALAISON] EXHALATION. — In his *Memoirs*, a consummate strategist, General Comte de Caprivi de Caprera de Montecuculli, Chancellor to Wilhelm II after Bismarck, wrote: "If one could avoid inadvertently exposing one's own troops to extermination, on the whole war would offer only advantages." And, in fact, must not the first principle of the military art consist in distinguishing friend from foe? Unfortunately, it is not unusual that, out of an excess of ardour, inattention, or ordinary clumsiness, we massacre our own and miss the adversary. According to official estimates, a reputable general will, in the course of a campaign of medium duration, eliminate two thirds of his effective forces. It is seemingly in vain that we endeavour to limit such regrettable errors by agreeing upon signs whereby belligerents can no longer be mistaken for one another. But changing uniforms, armbands or flags is an elementary ruse. For that reason it frequently rebounds upon its author. What is more, uniforms tend to resemble one another since their principal object is to merge into their surroundings. They are covered indistinguishably in leaves and mud. Position in itself has ceased to constitute a convincing item of intelligence because sudden movements of motorised units make it no longer possible to know for certain whether the enemy is in front of one or at one's rear. Any deep incursions or, as they say, *raids* into enemy territory bring with them analogous risks: is one not going to do away with precisely those prisoners or hostages one has happened to capture, indeed the secret agents, spies and sycophants one maintains at great expense and without whose action no victory is henceforth conceivable? The conclusion to be drawn from this preamble is evident: as long as we have not discovered the means of immunising ourselves from our own attacks, the combatant will remain the prey of a paralysing perplexity, the vigour of his morale and his fighting capacity will be reduced. Indeed one asks oneself whether the appearance of new, mechanically directed projectiles, whose point of impact, actual effect and ultimate destination still remain indeterminate, does not mark the end of the offensive spirit, which a glorious tradition has once and for all determined. What, to tell the truth, are the possibilities for exaltation in a war in which the blows are exchanged blindly? The importance of this question has not escaped the vigilance of General Staffs. It had already been grasped in high places that modern strategy was well on the way to becoming dispersed into confusion and abstraction. Like it or not, the future of war is linked to that of love, which the eugenists likewise dream of reducing to a pure communication at a distance. However, in each case, the element of physical contact continues, to prudent minds, to seem essential. As far as war, more particularly, is concerned, it is important that this contact be re-established at the earliest opportunity if we are to preserve for conflict its stimulus and its *raison d'être*.

Among the numerous scientists who have given their attention to this problem, some have been led to study closely the resources offered by odours as *recognition-signs*. That one might be able to recognise somebody by their odour does not astonish us: we know that our dogs recognise us in this way. But my dog does not recognise my brother or my cousin without ever having sniffed them, because my brother or my cousin do not have the same odour as myself. Among mammals the individual variations are too great. A man's personal odour provides a precise indication of his quantitative chemical nature, that is to say *his entire personality*. But the experiments of Huber and Sir John Lubbock on ants have made it possible

to establish that, individual variations being as near as may be nil, there exists *a family odour* by which ants from the same nest recognise each other, even after many months of separation. Let us emphasise that what we have here is not a phenomenon of memory: ants from the same nest, accustomed to their special odour, pay no attention to it, are not troubled by it and, when one presents them with one of their sisters, long separated from them, the odour of the newcomer does not concern them in the least. On the other hand, they are immediately shocked and irritated by the unusual odour of a stranger and punish it with death.

The import of these observations is plain. By applying with an increased rigour the rules of military discipline it is perfectly possible to suppress the individual variations among soldiers in the same army and, as a consequence, to unify their odour. By drilling, on the other hand, their sense of smell with an appropriate regime of training, one may by degrees teach them to recognise each other even in the darkness, whatever their appearance or dress might be. In this way the chances of mistakes will, for practical purposes, be eliminated, whereas keenness will be increased.

But a more complex problem remains to be solved: that of projectiles, which must be made selective, that is to say sensitive to odours. Here again we could usefully draw inspiration from certain scientific undertakings where applications have been crowned with success. Anxious to avoid maritime collisions and runnings aground, an inventor at the end of the last century envisaged the replacement of lighthouses, often hidden by fog, and sirens, often helpless to prevail over the noise of the waves, with smell-buoys which, by means of a special perfume, would point out to mariners their proper route.[66] It suffices, to achieve this end, to reverse the proposition. By providing the projectiles with a sort of olfactory organ, it will be relatively easy to direct them at will towards an enemy whose odour will act as a magnet or, on the contrary, render them inoffensive to friendly and allied soldiers (those having, thanks to a previously established international agreement, adopted the prescribed odour). The time is therefore not so far distant when, no longer exploding and scattering death at random, aerial torpedoes will come and settle amicably beside the combatant isolated in the night, like fraternal messages launched across space.

EXIGENCE. — It is easier to define moral exigency than to justify it. Everything is clear if one aspires to become a saint in order to obey the exigencies of God, or a hero to obey those of society, which is God. But suppose God, under his two aspects, collapses, what are the supposed values in whose name one stubbornly persists in governing or governing oneself? There remains only the inward exigency which impels the individual to offer himself as an example, that is to say the most vulgar form of ostentation.

EXISTENCE. — For some time now there has been a lot of talk about a managed economy. Definitions of this term vary according to the degree of premeditation each of the partisans of this method advocate.

But the efficacy of any system or theory having as its object the production and distribution of the necessary, as well as the superfluous, is in the last analysis determined by the merit and the probity of those who have conceived these theories or systems and those who apply them.

The impeccable organisation of individual existence is the basis of any serious community. Only the individual who is capable of imposing upon himself a plan and who carries it out with a meticulous rigour wins the right to establish plans for others.

It is within the power of anyone to organise their existence. Let them consult the model fixed once and for all by the Ten Commandments.

An existence thus regulated is never drab or routine. On the contrary, it is an exhilarating adventure in which one daily reaps new material rewards, but the spirit also finds its share.

[EXODE] EXODUS. — A kind of hymn or song intoned at the end of meals. The exodus was gay and frolicsome.[67]

EXOLETE.[68] — Assiduous priest at the Divine Service or puerile corollary. To be recognised, according to Ausonius, by its laboured clazomenae.

EXONIROSE.[69] — *Bot.* Rosaceous plant, exuding a white latex, also called *rose de songe*, dream rose, flowering for preference by night or at dawn. It possesses, like the Rose of Jericho or *jérose*, the curious property of reviving after having been dried. Not to be confused with the dog-rose or *rose cochonnière... C'est une pièce d'amour, tout distillée a l'exonirose des dames françaises* (It is a lovely thing, wholly distilled from the exoniroses of French womanhood), VOLTAIRE, *Lett. au pr. roy. de Pr.*, 1 June 1739. *Cueillons l'exonirose au matin de la vie* (Let us gather the exonirose in the morning of life), LAMARTINE, 2nd *Meditation*.

EXPIATION. — Willy Francis, a young Black from Louisiana who, at the age of fifteen, killed a pharmacist while robbing him of four dollars and a second-rate watch, was condemned to death. On the day of his execution, which had been fixed for 3 May 1946, the executioner and his assistants happening to be drunk, the electric chair did not work, and young Francis was taken back to his cell.

From then on the pleas for clemency on behalf of the adolescent multiplied, but the appeal was finally rejected by the Supreme Court. Willy Francis had, it must be added, declared that he was tired of living in a state of anxiety and wished to go to God. After a year's delay his wish was granted and he sat down in the electric chair at six o'clock (G.M.T.) on 9 May 1947. At ten past six he was declared dead. Almost five hundred persons, most of them white, were crowded outside the prison to await news of the execution.

The same day, after a long chase, the hopes of the police-officers sent in pursuit of Stanislas Wazelewsky, a dangerous murderer, aged twenty-two, who had escaped, his feet shackled, from the prison at Montauban, were at last crowned with success. A posse comprising eighty gendarmes, forty-five inspectors, some twenty armed peasants and numerous specially trained dogs was organised about the mansion belonging to Monsieur Prebasc, near Verlhac-Tescou. A police-trap was laid in the grounds of the mansion and, at about eleven-thirty the bandit made his appearance. "Who goes there?" The question remaining unanswered, three machine-guns opened fire and Wazelewsky collapsed, struck down by seven projectiles.

[EXPLICATION] EXPLANATION. — Nobody is unaware of the adverse situation of the devotees of Truth; they have so little influence that, so as not to cease to merit the confidence the vulgar herd place in them, they do not hesitate to make use of the most suspect of worldly illusions; and a shameful alliance between Progress and Truth has been celebrated.

I certainly do not presume to explain the reasons for this, but there is one instance I can point out which I flatter myself is not lacking in interest. This is the disappointment occasioned by the discovery of the paltry place man occupies in the universe.

After he had deprived God of the privilege of possessing the Truth, man had so high an opinion of himself that he knew no rest until the privilege in question had been awarded to himself: had he not accomplished a brilliant victory over the Almighty? When the momentary commotion had died down, he realised that, at the same time, he had lost his most precious illusion, that of the divinity's friendship; I shall not dwell on the metaphysical consequences of that loss, which have already long been the conversation of pedants, the subject of every other poem, and the delight of philosophers. To be sure science is not my line and, if I speak, I do not necessarily suppose that my reflections are worthy of your attention. You are free to find fault with my audacity, but you are answerable that I have chosen to run this risk and that, saving your reverence, I am not answerable to you.

That was an unprecedented defeat which the scientists endured when they hauled down the flag, faced with the Truth. To recognise that it is not, as they say in their barbaric vocabulary, anthropomorphic, is to recognise that the unit of measurement itself, man, is wanting and that, if he no longer fulfils this role, science loses its *raison d'être*. In his laboratory, the scientist represents the human mind and this role, which once was the most honourable, has become his shame, now that he must answer for the disorder which he slips, willingly or unwillingly, into his experiments. In days gone by, the production of a certain number of facts having been achieved, he was at liberty to make some observations and to assign to them a significance which, if nothing subsequently intervened to refute him, was regarded

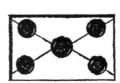 as a valid interpretation which made new advances possible and desirable. Today, to conclude is forbidden him, for his conclusions, as well as his observations, all bearing the stamp of

his personal genius, are thereby blemished with inexactitude. — And even his instruments, perfected organs, are now suspect.

We note, by way of parenthesis, the charming simplicity of certain persons who, as soon as reason falls into disfavour, enthrone foolishness, although it is rather unlikely that the disfavour of the one may not immediately entail that of the other.

I will certainly be taxed with cynicism; nevertheless the unfortunate situation in which science finds itself is rather diverting. I can't help it. As far as I'm concerned, everything that humbles man affords matter for laughter. If the scientist consents to resign his prerogatives, in return for that he is in no way deprived of the right to form hypotheses, crazy as they might be, on condition that, defended against criticism by a multitude of experiments, he shows they are not subject to the contingencies of chance. I often ask myself why this solution — which, in actual fact, is no more than a stopgap adopted for the lack of anything better — why everybody says it's so marvellous: no mention is made of the science called experimental without its triumph being celebrated.

It is far from being the case, though, that this supposed triumph, the consolation of the common herd distressed at the lugubrious aspect of the modern world, likewise consoles the scientists who — perfectly inevitable though they hold it to be — are none the less obliged to recognise that it is the reason the disorder they wished to avoid by this expedient is today pretty well at its highest point. How come? In vain has their vigilance constantly been on the alert; something always escapes it and if, unlikely as it may seem, by some wonder the list were complete, it would signal for that very reason the inauguration of the reign of confusion: what am I saying? the reign of confusion has already long been with us. The tangle of observations is inextricable. And any number of problems are insoluble only because the answer is lost in the labyrinth of documents.

I am not a humanist and, dismal as mankind's destitution might be, it matters little to me. It is entirely up to you to beg for mercy, like the dictator Sulla[70] when he abdicated his dictatorship; but take care that the universe does not promptly avenge itself on your vanity which allows you to believe that you merit its deference and respect.

[EXPOSITION] EXPOSURE/EXHIBITION.[71] — Act of abandoning a child on the public thoroughfare: *The exposure of children is cruel and customary among Christians.* LE MAITRE, *Plaid.* 7, in RICHELET. Deformed children are exposed as a matter of preference: *If they [the Spartans] found a child malformed, delicate and weak, and if they judged it would not be healthy and strong, they condemned it to perish and had it exposed.* ROLLIN, *Hist. anc. Oeuvres,* Vol. II, p.523. In the same way certain individuals called artists (see entry for that word) have a custom by which they place their works before the eye of the public when these are particularly distressing or ridiculous. In other words, they abandon their works to passers-by who, at the moment they take possession of the abandoned works, receive the title of art-lovers. But it quite often happens that none of the passers-by pass for an art-lover, the works thus placed leaving the passer-by who prefers to pass them by impassive. When this result is obtained, the artist experiences a splendid satisfaction and a legitimate pride, which is easy to understand since the work he has abandoned to the passer-by, have equally been abandoned by the latter; the exposure is double, and thus it counts as two. It suffices for an artist regularly to repeat this exploit for him to achieve fame. In order to expose without pause or repose, some even propose to the poor that they pose: this is an apotheosis. He who exposes is then the object of religious ceremonies called private views in the course of which he personally exposes himself to the vermin.

EXPRESSION.[72] — Bird song being, as we know, of Orphic origin, it is perfectly legitimate to consider it as a properly human means of expression. What, in fact, would remain of it if men did not exist to hear and interpret it? True bird song is that which the poets (sic) untiringly sing but, among those latter, daring innovators no longer hesitate to substitute for classical paraphrase in plain language a literal transcription according to the principal principle set forth by Charles Dickens in the Animal Alphabet. In this way Lenz has noted eighteen different songs of the chaffinch, to which he gave distinct names. Here are the main ones:

1. The Schmalkalde reduplication: *tzitzitzitzi tzitzitzitzitzitzitzitzirrrrenttzaipiah, tololololozisss-coutziah.* This song is, as we can see, interrupted by a pause and ends in a ringing manner.

2. The piercing song of wine: *tzitzitzi-willillilltih, dappldappldappl de wingihai.*

3. The unpleasant song of wine: *tzitzitzitzi-llillillrllillisjibsjbsj iwihdrai.*

4. Pine-oil: *tzitzitzitzitzirrrrezwoifzwoifzwoifz-oiffihdrai.*

5. The crazy happy-new-year: *tititititi totozaipeutziah.*

6. The happy-new-year in Harz: *tzitziwillwilwillwillsaispeutziah.*

7. The common happy-new-year: *tzitzitzitziwihaiwihaiwihaizaispeutziah.*

8. The common cavalcade: *tzitzitzitzirrrrihtjobjobjobairoitihe.*

9. The cavalier: *tzitzitzitzitzitzizullullull-iobjobjobjaireitjah.*

10. The glass: *tzitzizeutzeuzeuwollillilli-woftziah.*

Certain remarks have also been made on the subject of sparrows. These creatures, chatterers if ever there be such, utter a *dieb, dieb* when flying, and *schlip, schlip* when they are perched. At rest, or when eating, we hear a continual repeating *bilp* or *bioum* is always audible. *Durr* and *di, di, di* are their cries of tenderness. *Terr*, pronounced forcibly and rolling the *rr* indicates the approach of a danger. If the danger increases, they utter a cry which can be noted: *telterelteltel.* When the time comes for fights for possession of the females, the males emit the sounds *tel, tel, spli, del, del, dieb, schlik* etc., which pour from their throats in a noise often deafening and disagreeable.

This notation of bird song is very difficult to understand. It is, however, very widespread in works on ornithology. We give here a few examples which are of interest in showing how birds assemble letters.

The tree-creeper pours forth a vivacious *tsig-tsig, tsig-tsig.*
The missel-thrush: *trai-trai, trai-trai.*
The magpie: *plieu, plieu.*
The amorous chaffinch sings: *tchi-tchi-tchi-rah-i-ts... iu.* To which the female responds: *si-si-si*, and together they repeat *trr-trr-trr.*
Cry of the female oriole: *yoo-yio-yo-o.*

The male oriole begins with *hi-de-lu* and continues *hi-de-lu-a-i-a*.

The song of the nightingale was noted by Dureau de La Malle thus:

Tinu, tinu, tinu, tiau
Spretiu, z-qua,
Querrec, pi, pi,
Tid, tio, tio, tix,
Qutio, qutio, qutio, qu'-tio,
Zquo, zquo, zquo, zquo
Zi, zi, zi, zi, zi, zi, zi,
Querrer, tiu, aquiz, pi, pi, qui.

As long ago as 1787, the journal *Les Affiches de Senlis* had provided this phonic reproduction of the nightingale's song:

Tiuu, tiuu, tiuu, tiuu,
Lpay tiuu zqua;
Quorror pipu
Tio, tio, tio, tio, tix;
Qutio, qutio, qutio, qutio,
Zquo, zquo, zquo, zquo,
Zi, zi, zi, zi, zi, zi, zi,
Quorror tiuu zqua pipiqui.

Spoken by an Italian, this imitation is, it seems remarkable. Professor Isidore Isou is a past master at this kind of exercise.

[EXTASE] ECSTASY. — Sensibility in a pure state, deprived of any intelligible element, reduced to the condition of a sewer in which rapidly flowing waters converge (but the sewer is a bottomless chasm); sentiment of evasion and of infinite hilarity in which absurdity runs riot and abandons itself, with its contrary, to instantaneous exchanges which go astray in space. Joy that is insupportable, useless, impossible — and joyless.

[EXTASIEE] ECSTATIC. — On the night of 23 October 1816, the *curé* of Lignan and others, being in the room of Marie-Ange, who was in ecstasy, heard the kisses imprinted on her lips by Our Lord and Our Beloved Mother and recorded that each kiss produced a small quantity of fluid which Marie-Ange swallowed. When she had swallowed a fair quantity, the kisses continuing, she allowed some fluid to escape from one corner of her mouth. The *curé* then approaching, he gathered it up with his finger and swallowed it. When he had swallowed a fair quantity, the kisses continuing, he gave a lick thereof to each person who was in the room. The kisses continuing, and the fluids still escaping from the lips of Marie-Ange, the *curé* had the persons who were in the kitchen come upstairs; all tasted it and found it delicious. The *curé* soaked a white handkerchief of Rouen linen in that fluid, which I possess, along with relics of Marie-Ange... The kisses beginning anew...

More ardent than ordinary kisses, the loud kisses the young girl received were often each accompanied by a pretty bon-bon. It might be said that never had a saint been seen or known to have received from Our Lord and his divine mother so many kisses as Marie-Ange! As the letters she received said, Marie-Ange was the veritable spouse of the Song of Songs: is it any wonder, then, that she received kisses? We should rather see in those kisses the irrefragable proof of what the letters affirm.

One day in July 1817, at Cazouls, in the room of the *curé* Monsieur Julien, we were eight persons; Marie-Ange was in ecstasy, and we heard the kisses on her lips. We approached, and we saw that each kiss produced in her mouth a bon-bon the size of a pea. She received nearly a hundred. When her tongue was covered in these, Marie-Ange extended it; and what was our astonishment at seeing those bon-bons, of all colours, set out in line in an admirable manner.

APPENDIX I. — *The first supplemement to the* Da Costa, *published in February 1948, began with this unsigned text.*

ANONYMITY. — There is perhaps some point in devoting a few lines to an enterprise today fallen into abeyance: the *Da Costa Encyclopédique*. Its most grievous fault (there were plenty of others) was no doubt to be founded upon a fairly uncompromising anonymity. It took the risk of having done with those signatures which flaunt themselves on every picture and at the end of every text, to the point of constituting, *de facto*, their sole exchange-value. That programme was undoubtedly far too arrogant, and the position it indicated was soon judged untenable. The collaborators in the *Da Costa Encyclopédique* before long reckoned themselves more directly conspicuous in their anonymity than the late Monsieur Valéry, present at the Sorbonne at the elucidation of his own verses. Was that once again the finger of God, the eye of conscience? Each of them wound up considering himself personally responsible not only for what he had written but also, equally, for the entire enterprise and the corpus of misunderstandings it threatened to engender. It was a perfect outbreak of scruples.

How can such a warning be regarded as negligible? Let us then set out this principle: one signs an article in a review, less to pride oneself on being its author than to distinguish oneself from all the others. For that reason only a qualified anonymity will be observed here. We put this backsliding on record, but let it not be imagined that one is so easily let off the hook as regards the anonymity that remains the most stirring of watchwords, the only one capable of inciting us to pronounce, come what may, the final rejoinders in a dialogue that is coming to an end.

APPENDIX II. — (Translators & Order of publication): *All translations are by Iain White except those indicated by* *: *Annette Michelson,* ‡: *Dominic Faccini,* ¶: *John Harman. This list gives the original order of publication of the texts in* Documents; *volume I appeared in 1929, volume II in 1930.*

Volume I, no. 2: ‡Architecture, ‡Nightingale; no. 3: Absolute, ¶Materialism, ¶Metaphor; no. 4: Black Birds, Man (1), Eye (1, ¶2, 3 & 4); no. 5: Camel, Cults, Man (2), Misfortune, Dust, Reptiles, ¶Talkie; no. 6: *Slaughterhouse, *Factory Chimney, Crustaceans, Metamorphosis (1, 2 & *3); no. 7: Spittle (‡1 & ‡2), Debacle, Formless.

Volume II, no. 1: Space, Hygiene; no. 2: Pensum, Threshold, Work; no. 4: Benga, Aesthete, Keaton, Pottery; no. 5: Bonjour (Brothers), ¶Mouth, *Museum; no. 6: Angel, Ju-ju, Kali; no. 7: Skyscraper, Sun.

The Related Texts *appeared as follows:*

Volume I, no. 4: ¶Civilisation, *Human Face; no. 6: ¶Big Toe; Volume II, no. 1: ‡Gunshot.

The Da Costa *is translated by Iain White except for the following entries, which are by Alexis Lykiard:*

Eglise, Ejaculation, Erotisme (A to Z), *Evidence.*

APPENDIX III. — (Biographies): *All biographies are by Dominique Lecoq except those indicated by *: Alastair Brotchie, ¶: Malcolm Green, ‡: from information provided by Michel Waldberg.*

GEORGES AMBROSINO (1912-1984). — A physicist, Ambrosino devoted himself to the study of the atomic structure of matter and worked with the *Commissariat à l'énergie atomique*. As a philosopher he displayed a universal curiosity, and even instructed Lacan on Hegel. Along with his fellow-pupil from the *Lycée Chaptal*, René Chénon, he joined the *Cercle Communiste Démocratique* where he met Bataille. He then took part in *Contre-Attaque,* and after its dissolution, joined the secret society Acéphale. In 1937 he was one of the founders, with Bataille, Caillois and Klossowski, of the *Collège de Sociologie*. After the war, Ambrosino wrote scientific articles for *Critique* and was a guiding informant to Bataille in the writing of *The Accursed Share* ("This book," Bataille wrote, "is also largely the work of Ambrosino.")

JACQUES BARON (1905-1986). — Baron started early as a poet: he published his first poems in 1921 in *Aventure* and participated in the Dada movement. In 1921 he met Breton and joined the Surrealists. He broke with Breton in 1929, became one of the editors of *Documents* and joined the *Cercle Communiste Démocratique;* Boris Souvarine said of him: "he was at the origin of my relations with André Breton and his entourage." To earn a living Baron became a merchant sailor, then a radio-journalist. He published many collections of poems, among them *L'Allure poétique,* and a novel, *Charbon de mer,* some memoirs, *L'An 1 du Surréalisme,* and collaborated on such reviews as *Le Voyage en Grèce, La Critique sociale* and *Minotaure.*

GEORGES BATAILLE **(1897-1962).** — (Note: This biography concerns itself only with social references. It says nothing about the agony of Bataille's life or his experience of the impossible. He relied on literature to transmit its sense, and to the reader wishing to receive that message I recommend his works.)

Georges Bataille was born in Billom, a small medieval town east of Clermont-Ferrand, the second son of a syphilitic father who had gone blind and was to become paralysed. He left the Auvergne at an early age, when his family moved to Reims in 1900. He was a dreadful student at the *lycée* in that town, the *lycée* where some years later the founding members of the *Grand Jeu* group came together (Daumal, Gilbert-Lecomte, Vailland). In 1914, Mme Bataille left her husband when the town was threatened with bombardment by German artillery, and fled with her son to her remaining family at Riom-ès-Montagnes. The father died alone the following year. In 1916 Bataille was called up, but his illness caused him to be definitively rejected by the army. He thought of taking up an ecclesiastical career and in 1917 enrolled at the Saint-Flour seminary where he spent one year. He then published the first text bearing his name: a six page pamphlet entitled *Notre-Dame de Rheims*. But he gave up the seminary, and moved to Paris where he entered the Ecole des Chartes, the school for the study of ancient documents. In 1920 he spent some time in London, where he met the philosopher Henri Bergson, and a visit to Quarr Abbey on the Isle of Wight put an end to any idea of a religious vocation. He left the Ecole with a brilliant thesis, and became an archivist/palaeographer at the Bibliothèque nationale in 1922. In the same year he was sent to Madrid to the Ecole des hautes études hispaniques, and fell in love with bull-fighting.

From 1923 to 1925, he was close to Leon Chestov and worked with him on the translation into French of his book *The Idea of Goodness in Tolstoy and Nietzsche*. The Russian philosopher had a profound influence on Bataille; this being the period when Bataille discovered the works of Nietzsche and of Freud. He took a lively interest in the problems of translating into French the concepts of psychoanalysis. At this time he also started lifelong friendships, first with the ethnologist Alfred Métraux, then with Michel Leiris, André Masson the painter, and Theodore

Fraenkel. His meeting with André Breton resulted in mutual hostility. Apart from one single anonymous contribution to *La Révolution surréaliste* (a transcription into modern French of *fatrasies*, absurd medieval poems), he kept apart from the Surrealist movement.

In 1926 Bataille underwent an analysis with Doctor Adrien Borel: it was brief, as was the practice of those days. After the analysis, he could at last write. First a text entitled *WC*, whose manuscript he destroyed, then *L'anus solaire*, which was published in 1931 with illustrations by André Masson, and *L'Histoire de l'oeil*, published in 1928 under the pseudonym of Lord Auch — an abbreviation for *Aux chiottes...!* [On the shit-hole]. Alongside this black erotic writing, Bataille was active as a numismatist, writing articles for scholarly reviews such as *Aréthuse*, or *La République des Lettres, des Sciences et des Arts*. In 1929 he was one of the founders of the review *Documents* in which he attempted the impossible: to put official science up against texts that radically questioned it. The review was closed down by its owner at the beginning of 1931. The editorial board brought together Georges Bataille and a number of dissident Surrealists; they further collaborated in publishing *Un cadavre*, a pamphlet directed against André Breton.

In 1928 Bataille married Sylvia Maklès who became a famous actress (she was directed by Jean Renoir in *Une Partie de Campagne*, and Georges Bataille appears as an extra in the film dressed as... a priest!). They had one daughter, Laurence, born in 1930, who became a highly-regarded psychoanalyst. In 1934 Bataille separated from his wife, though they were not officially divorced until 1946. Sylvia then married the psychoanalyst Jacques Lacan and Georges married Diane Kotchoubey de Beauharnais, with whom he had a daughter, Julie. The two couples continued friendly relations based on mutual esteem: Lacan invited Bataille in the late fifties to contribute to the seminar he held at the Hôpital Saint-Anne.

In 1931, Bataille was a member of Boris Souvarine's *Cercle Communiste Démocratique*, and contributed to the review *La Critique Sociale* where he published important articles including *La notion de dépense* and, with Raymond Queneau, *Critique des fondements de la dialectique hégélienne*. From 1934 he followed Alexandre Kojève's famous lectures on Hegel. That year, he started a liaison with Colette Peignot who was then the companion of Souvarine. He reacted with implacable hatred towards Bataille which he maintained up until his last writings (in 1984) where he inveighs against him as a "sexual lunatic," and an "acephalous writer fixated on an apparently cosmic anus."

In the mid-thirties, Bataille began an activity imposed by the danger of fascism: he created the *Contre-Attaque* movement which was joined by Breton and his friends, but dissolved in 1936. The following year he founded the secret society called Acéphale, took part in the creation and organisation of the *Société de psychologie collective* which included both anthropologists and psychoanalysts, and with Leiris and Caillois set up the College of Sociology which assembled some remarkable minds, among them Theodor Adorno and Walter Benjamin (whose manuscripts were hidden by Bataille in the Bibliothèque nationale during the war).

Colette Peignot's death in 1938 shook him for some time. He wrote *Le Coupable*, *L'Expérience intérieure* and *Madame Edwarda* which was published in 1940 under the pseudonym of Pierre Angélique. He met Maurice Blanchot "to whom he was bound immediately with admiration and agreement." He became ill and left the Bibliothèque nationale in 1942, then moved out of Paris to Vezelay. That year he published *Le Petit* under the pseudonym of Louis Trente.

In 1946 he founded the review *Critique* which is still in existence and he published in its pages numerous critical articles which were collected in several of his books such as *La Part maudite* or *Le Littérature et le mal*. In 1958 Bataille made one last attempt to start a review: he put together a contents list for *Genèse* with the help of Patrick Waldberg, but the publisher Maurice Girodias cancelled the project. In the course of the fifties several works appeared which had been written earlier, such as *L'Abbé C*, *Le Bleu du ciel*, and also *Lascaux ou la naissance de l'art*, and *Manet*.

Bataille ran out of money and was forced to take up employment again: in 1949 he became librarian at Carpentras, in Provence, then in 1951 at Orléans which he left in 1962 for a job at the Bibliothèque nationale, which however, his illness and then death prevented him from taking up. Suffering increasingly badly from arteriosclerosis, he had managed to finish *Les Larmes d'Eros* (1961) the last book published in his lifetime. He had planned to re-work *La Part maudite*, but died in Paris on 8 July 1962, he is buried in Vezelay. Two further books appeared posthumously: *Ma Mère*, which was its author's first commercial success, and *Le Mort*.

JACQUES-ANDRÉ BOIFFARD (1902-1961). — Boiffard began medical studies, which he broke off in 1924 after a meeting with André Breton arranged for him by Pierre Naville, a friend from his youth. He dedicated himself thereafter entirely to Surrealist researches, participated in the work of the *Bureau des recherches surréalistes* and wrote the preface to the first number of *La Révolution surréaliste*. However, not much attracted to literature, he turned to photography and became Man Ray's assistant. His photographs of Nancy Cunard date from this period, as do the shots of Paris taken in 1928 that accompany André Breton's *Nadja*. That same year he was abruptly expelled from the Surrealist movement after taking a series of photographs of Simone Breton. In 1930, with Bataille, Leiris, Limbour et al., he contributed to *Un cadavre*, the pamphlet attacking André Breton. His best known photographs appeared in *Documents*. Boiffard then joined forces with Eli Lotar, and received financial assistance from Georges-Henri Rivière and the Vicomte de Noailles. The two photographers set out on a world tour, accompanied by a rich Spaniard: the venture was a flop and came to a halt in Tangier. In the thirties, a time of hectic political conflict, Boiffard was a member of the *Octobre* group, led by the Prévert brothers, and showed his work in the exhibitions of the *Association des Ecrivains et Artistes Révolutionnaires*. When his father died, in 1935, he resumed his studies and gained his doctorate in medicine in 1940. Boiffard then specialised in radiology: it was to be his last relationship with photography.

*JACQUES BRUNIUS (1906-1967). — Poet, collagist, actor, *cinéaste*, translator, radio broadcaster for the BBC. Brunius was active in the Surrealist movement from the thirties when he worked in the cinema with the Prévert brothers and contributed to *Minotaure*. He lived in London from 1940 and ran French programming on BBC radio, and he was also the English editor of the exiled journal and publishing house *Fontaine* (Algiers). Between 1941 and 1945 he was the broadcaster and author of the radio programme *Ici Londres: Les Voix de la liberté*. He wrote a biography of William Beckford and a study of Lewis Carroll and was a prolific translator of Saki, Carroll, and various other English authors and playwrights (Pinter, Dylan Thomas). He continued as a broadcaster on the French service of the BBC until 1963. In the late fifties he made futile attempts to revive Surrealism in the UK, the official group having ceased activities in 1947, but died on the eve of the Exeter Surrealist exhibition of 1967 which he had helped to organise. Author of several hundred articles on aspects of cinema under at least half a dozen pseudonyms. He lived in Paris and London alternately after the war, and remained loyal to Breton's faction during the "Carrouges affair," unlike most of the other ex-members of the English group and, indeed, the Da Costas.

JACQUES CHAVY (b. 1912). — An architect by training, and translator of art books (from English and German into French). Participated in the *"Amis de Monde"* with Henri Barbusse, the *Cercle Communiste Démocratique* with Boris Souvarine and Bataille, in *Contre-Attaque* with Bataille and Breton, then in the secret society Acéphale and the *Collège de Sociologie*. He was the managing editor of the review *Acéphale* and contributed many articles to *Critique* and the *Da Costa*.

RENÉ CHENON (1912-1993). — A fellow pupil of Ambrosino's at the *Lycée Chaptal* in Paris, René Chenon followed a career as a professor of mathematics, interrupted only by five years captivity during the war. He met Bataille while a member of Souvarine's *Cercle Communiste Démocratique*, and left with Bataille to become a member of Acéphale.

ARNAUD DANDIEU (1897-1933). — Dandieu initially studied law and became a solicitor's clerk before taking up a post at the Bibliothèque Nationale in 1925. There he met Bataille, with whom he had many discussions: deeply Catholic, interested in philosophy, psychopathology, epistemology and sociology, Dandieu contributed to many reviews: *Documents*, but also *Europe, Mouvements, Esprit, La Revue Mondiale, La Revue d'Allemagne*. In 1930, with Robert Aron, he founded the movement *Ordre Nouveau*, which denounced the vulgar materialism at work in liberal societies. The two men published a book-length manifesto entitled *Le Cancer américain;* a second followed, *La Révolution nécessaire* (1933) to which Bataille contributed anonymously. Dandieu also published a collection of poems and an essay on Proust. He died prematurely, of complications following a minor operation.

ROBERT DESNOS (1900-1945). — Primarily a poet, his first works appeared in 1917, two years before he met Benjamin Péret, who introduced him to the Paris Dada group and to André Breton. He was an active member of the Surrealist group while remaining a journalist on *Paris-Soir*. After splitting with the Surrealists, he joined Bataille and *Documents* and was one of the authors of *Un cadavre* which attacked *"le boeuf Breton."* His career in radio began in 1932, and he became friendly with Artaud, Picasso, and also Hemingway and John Dos Passos. A lover of music, especially jazz, and of cinema, he wrote many critical texts on film as well as numerous scenarios. He was active in the Resistance during the war; and was arrested in 1944 and deported to Buchenwald, then Térézine, where he died of exhaustion following typhus a few weeks after the camp's liberation. He wrote for many reviews, including *Littérature, La Révolution surréaliste*, and *Variétés*. His principal publications include various poetry collections and three novels, the first two being available in English from Atlas Press: *Deuil pour deuil* (1924), *La Liberté ou l'amour!* (1927) and *Le vin est tiré* (1943).

CHARLES DUITS (1921-1991). — A writer, born in Paris of Dutch/American parents who had emigrated to the USA, and therefore of American citizenship. He met Breton in New York during the war where he had returned to study at Harvard. His role in the *Da Costa* was important since he did not hesitate to re-write various texts in order to accentuate their provocative nature. He published many novels, including erotica, and a memoir of Breton curiously entitled: *André Breton a-t-il dit passe...*

¶**CARL EINSTEIN (1885-1940).** — One of the most important writers and art/literary theorists of his time. His "cubist" novel *Bebuquin*, published in 1912, was highly influential for Dada and illuminated his call for an end to the realistic or psychological novel. He published one of the first monographs on African art, *Negro Sculpture* (1915), and his *Art of the 20th Century* (1926) was equally important. In 1919 he co-edited two of the most political of the Dada journals with Grosz, periodicals that fiercely attacked the spirit of the Weimar republic, which he abandoned for France in 1928. In Paris, apart from co-editing *Documents*, he collaborated on Jolas' *Transition*, wrote a major work on Braque and the screenplay to Jean Renoir's *Toni*. In 1936 he left for Spain where he fought with the legendary anarchist Durutti Column. He was arrested for his part in the civil war on returning to France and committed suicide in 1940 when he realised he would be unable to escape from Fascist persecution after the German invasion.

*JEAN FERRY (1906-1976). — Born Jean Levy, he contributed to Surrealist reviews (*Minotaure, Documents 34* etc.) under that name before the war when, for obvious reasons, he changed it to Ferry. He worked in the cinema with the Prévert brothers and the October group, stayed in Paris during the war and fought with the resistance during the liberation of the city. He wrote short stories (*Le Mécanicien et autres contes*, 1950, prefaced by Breton), several studies of Roussel, screenplays (including that of *Malpertuis*), even acted in various films. His association with Surrealism lasted between 1932 and 1950 when he joined the College of Pataphysics, in which he played a major role until his death.

MARCEL GRIAULE (1898-1956). — A linguist by training, turned ethnologist, between 1928 and 1929 Griaule conducted fieldwork in Ethiopia, whence he returned with a curious and magnificent book, *Silhouettes et graffitis abyssins*, published in 1933 with an introduction by Marcel Mauss. On his return he joined the *Documents* team as sub-editor (at the same time as Michel Leiris) and, backed by Rivet and Rivière, organised the ethnographic expedition which, starting in 1931, he led from Dakar to Djibouti, the aim of which, in addition to gathering ethnographic data, was to augment the collections of the Musée du Trocadéro. Michel Leiris accompanied the expedition as secretary-archivist. In the course of the mission Griaule encountered the Dogon of the Bandiagara cliff-faces, a people that became the chief object of his researches. In 1942 he was elected to the first chair of general ethnology at the Sorbonne. Among other writings he published *Les Masques Dogons* (1938), *Dieu d'eau, entretien avec Ogotemmêli* (1948), and finally, *Renard pâle, ethnologie des Dogons,* in collaboration with Germaine Dieterlen.

*ROBERT LEBEL (1904-1984). — Lebel first met Breton in 1930 but his involvement with Surrealism really began in New York during the war. He was active in the movement until the late fifties. A writer on art principally, he was especially close to Duchamp and wrote the first monograph on him. His fiction, although infrequent, was quite outstanding, in particular *L'Inventeur du temps gratuit* which first appeared in *Le Surréalisme, même* in 1957. His son, Jean-Jacques Lebel, also a contributor to the *Da Costa* (**Et cetera**.) was born in 1936; a painter, poet and polemicist, he was actively involved in the events of May '68, and was a promoter of happenings and translator of the American poets of the time.

MICHEL LEIRIS (1901-1990). — Having taken his *baccalauréat* in philosophy in 1918, Leiris made half-hearted beginnings in the study of chemistry but showed more interest in jazz, which he was discovering at that time. Between 1921 and 1924 there came a series of decisive meetings: Max Jacob, Georges-Henri Rivière, Jean Dubuffet, André Masson, Robert Desnos, Georges Bataille. A Surrealist in 1924, he broke with Breton in 1929. Meanwhile he had married Louise Godon, step-daughter of Picasso's dealer Daniel-Henri Kahnweiler, travelled in Egypt and Greece, and written his first book, *Aurora* (published in English by Atlas Press). He joined the *Documents* team as sub-editor, and left in 1930 to become the secretary-archivist in the ethnographic mission Marcel Griaule led from Dakar to Djibouti. This experience furnished material for the unclassifiable *Afrique fantôme* (1934), a book which brought about the definitive break with Griaule and which was pulped in 1941 on the orders of the Vichy government. In November 1937, in response to the current international situation, he decided, with Bataille and Roger Caillois, to found the *Collège de Sociologie*. He took part, in 1945, in an important mission to the Ivory Coast which led, as a result of the report it submitted to parliament, to the suppression of forced labour in the French African colonies. Along with his activities as a research-worker with the *Centre national de la recherche scientifique*, he was a member with Sartre, of the editorial committee of *Les Temps modernes* and was involved in various political struggles, notably against the war in Algeria. In 1966 Leiris became friendly with Francis Bacon, on whose painting he published numerous texts. His powerfully original work partakes, on the one hand, of literature — albeit "considered as a bull fight," and it takes in autobiography, as in *L'Age d'homme, La Règle du jeu,* art criticism, as in *Au Verso des images* or *Francis Bacon face et profil,* and music criticism, as in *Operratiques*. Equally it incorporates science, as in *La Langue secrète des Dogons de Saga* or *Race et civilisation*.

ELI LOTAR (1905-1969). — A Romanian by birth, son of a celebrated poet, his "official" name was Eliazar Lotar Teodoresco. In 1926 he became a French citizen and the companion of the German photographer Germaine Krull. He frequented cinematic circles — those of René Clair and, in particular, Luis Buñuel, with whom he remained friendly. Lotar published his photographs in Carlo Rim's review *Jazz, Variétés, Bifur* and *Documents*. The reportage on the slaughterhouses of La Villette remains one of his major works: it was closely akin to Bataille's current preoccupations. Lotar took part in many exhibitions alongside André Kertesz and Germaine Krull. After involvement in the theatre with Antonin Artaud and Roger Vitrac and with the *Octobre* group, he worked as a set-photographer or as a cameraman in many films with Jacques Brunius, Joris Ivens, Paul Painlevé, and Jean Renoir. He was assistant to Marc Allégret and director of three films, one of which, *Aubervilliers,* was chosen for the Cannes festival in 1946. His final years were particularly sombre, supported by the friendship of Giacometti who took Lotar as a model for his later sculptures.

ZDENKO REICH.— Biographical details remain few: before publishing in *Documents* he was a part of the *Grand Jeu* group centred around the magazine edited by René Daumal, Roger Vailland and Roger Gilbert-Lecomte.

‡**ISABELLE WALDBERG (1911-1990) & PATRICK WALDBERG (1913-1985)**. — Isabelle was born Margaretha Farner in Switzerland. A sculpture student in Zurich between 1933 and 1935 she came to Paris in 1938 and met Patrick Waldberg, and through him the other members of Acéphale, of which she was one of the two female members. Patrick Waldberg was born in Santa Monica of Irish immigrant parentage; both his parents died while he was still a boy. Educated in France he moved in leftist and Surrealist circles in the early thirties and met Bataille in Souvarine's *Cercle Communiste Démocratique*. His political activities caused his expulsion from France (he was an American citizen), but in 1937 he returned to France, joined Acéphale and became the secretary of the *Collège de Sociologie*. He volunteered for the French Army in 1939, was demobilised in late 1940, and joined the American forces; he fought in Algeria and from Normandy to Paris. He was a founder of the Voice of America. Both Waldbergs returned to Paris after the war, Isabelle holding numerous exhibitions, Patrick writing, chiefly on art, and splitting with Breton over the "Carrouges affair" in 1951.

APPENDIX IV. — (References & Bibliography): *English books are published in London, French in Paris, unless indicated otherwise. Section A is intended as a complete list of book-length translations of Bataille into English, whether currently available or not, the other sections list titles cited or consulted.*

A. GEORGES BATAILLE, ENGLISH TRANSLATIONS.

1. *L'Abbé C,* trans. Philip Facey, Marion Boyars, 1983.
2. *The Absence of Myth, Writings on Surrealism,* ed. & trans. Michael Richardson, Verso Books, 1994.
3. *The Accursed Share,* Zone Books, New York, Vol. I, 1988; Vols. II & III, 1993.
4. *Blue of Noon,* trans. Harry Mathews, US: Urizen Books, NY, 1978; UK: Marion Boyars, 1979.
5. *Eroticism,* trans. Mary Dalwood, John Calder, 1962; Marion Boyars, 1987.
6. *Guilty,* trans. Bruce Boone, Lapis Press, Los Angeles, 1988.
7. *The Impossible,* trans. Robert Hurley, City Lights, San Francisco, 1991.
8. *Inner Experience,* trans. Leslie A. Boldt, State University of New York Press, 1988.
9. *Lascaux, or the Birth of Art,* trans. Austryn Wainhouse, US: Skira, NY, 1955; UK: Macmillan, 1980.
10. *Literature and Evil,* trans. Alastair Hamilton, Calder & Boyars, 1973.
11. *Madame Edwarda,* trans. Austryn Wainhouse (as *The Naked Beast at Heaven's Gate*), Olympia Press, Paris, 1953.
12. *Manet,* trans. Austryn Wainhouse & James Emmons, US: Skira, NY, 1955; UK: Macmillan, 1983.
13. *My Mother,* trans. Austryn Wainhouse, US: Grove Press, San Francisco, 1972; UK: Cape, 1972.
14. *On Nietzsche,* trans. Bruce Boone, Athlone Press, 1992.
15. *The Story of the Eye,* trans. Austryn Wainhouse (as *A Tale of Satisfied Desire*), Olympia Press, Paris, 1953.
16. *The Story of the Eye,* trans. Joachim Neugroschel, US: Urizen Books, NY, 1977; UK: Marion Boyars, 1979; Penguin Books, 1982.
17. *The Tears of Eros,* trans. Peter Connor, City Lights, San Francisco, 1989.
18. *Theory of Religion,* trans. Robert Hurley, Zone Books, NY, 1989.
19. *The Trial of Gilles de Rais,* trans. Richard Robinson, Amok, Los Angeles, 1991.
20. *Visions of Excess, Selected Writings, 1927-1939,* ed. Allan Stoeckl, UK: Manchester University Press, 1985; USA: University of Minnesota Press, 1985.
21. Jolas, Eugène [ed.], *Vertical,* Gotham Bookmart Press, New York, 1941. Includes the *Manifesto* [in A22, 9-11]; Bataille, *The Sacred Conspiracy* (from *Acéphale,* 1); Caillois, *Ambiguity of the Sacred*; Duthuit, *For a Sacred Art* and a selection of Masson's drawings from *Acéphale.*
22. Hollier, Denis [ed.], *The College of Sociology,* University of Minnesota Press, 1988.

B. GEORGES BATAILLE, FRENCH TEXTS.

1. Bataille, Georges, *Oeuvres complètes,* Gallimard (12 volumes published between 1970 and 1988).

C. ON *DOCUMENTS.*

1. *Documents,* (reprinted in two volumes), Jean-Michel Place, 1991.
2. Bataille, Georges, *Programme* [B1, vol. II, 273].
3. Bataille, Georges, *Instructions pour la rencontre en forêt,* [B1, vol. II, 277-8].
4. Clifford, James, *The Predicament of Culture, Twentieth Century Ethnography, Literature & Art,* Harvard University Press,

Cambridge, Mass., 1988.

5. Lecoq, Dominique, *Documents, Acéphale, Critique: Bataille autour des revues*, in *Georges Bataille, Actes du colloque d'Amsterdam*, June 1985, Jan Versteeg [ed.], pp.117-130.

6. Leiris, Michel, *From the Impossible Bataille to the Impossible Documents*, in *Brisées: Broken Branches*, trans. Lydia Davis, North Point Press, San Francisco, 1989 (first published in *Critique* [E5]).

7. *A Documents Dossier*, special issue of *October*, 60, MIT Press, Cambridge, Mass., 1992.

D. ON ACÉPHALE.

1. *Acéphale* (reprint of the magazine), Jean-Michel Place, 1980.

2. Masson, André, *Le soc de la charrue*, in *Critique* [E5].

E. ON GEORGES BATAILLE.

1. Hollier, Denis, *Against Architecture, The Writings of Georges Bataille*, trans. Betsy Wing, MIT Press, Cambridge, Mass., 1992.

2. Kojève, Alexandre, *Introduction to the Reading of Hegel*, assembled by Raymond Queneau, edited by Allan Bloom, translated by James Nichols, Cornell University Press, 1980.

3. Richardson, Michael, *Georges Bataille*, Routledge, 1994.

4. Surya, Michel, *Georges Bataille, La Mort à l'Œuvre*, Séguier, 1987.

5. Various, *Hommage à Georges Bataille* [ed. Barthes, Deguy, Foucault], special issue of *Critique*, 195-6, August /September 1963, reprinted 1991.

6. Various, *Violent Silence, Celebrating Georges Bataille*, ed. Paul Buck (no publisher given), London, 1984.

7. Various, special issue of *October*, 36, MIT Press, Cambridge, Mass., 1986.

8. Various, *On Bataille*, ed. Allan Stoeckl, Yale French Studies, 78, New Haven, Connecticut, 1990.

9. Various, *Dossier Georges Bataille* [ed. Dominique Lecoq], special issue of *Magazine littéraire*, 243, June 1987.

F. ON THE *DA COSTA*.

1. Anon. Introduction to *Escrocs*, Cymbalum 'Pataphysicum, *Coll. Les Astéronymes*, 3, 1979.

2. Caradec, François & Arnaud, Noël, *Encyclopédie des farces et attrapes et des mystifications*, Pauvert, 1964.

3. Mesens, E.L.T. (ed.), *London Gallery News*, London Gallery, December 1946.

4. Mesens, E.L.T. (ed.), *London Gallery Express*, London Gallery, March-April 1947.

5. Waldberg, Isabelle & Patrick, *Un Amour Acéphale, Correspondence 1940-1949*, Eds. de la Différence, 1992.

G. ON THE *COLLÈGE DE 'PATAPHYSIQUE*.

1. Anon. *L'Histoire du Collège de 'Pataphysique* in *Monitoires du Cymbalum 'Pataphysicum*, 1, 14 July 1985.

2. Launoir, Ruy, *Clefs pour la 'Pataphysique*, Seghers, 1969.

3. Thomas, Henri, *Une saison volée*, Gallimard, 1986.

H. OTHER.

1. Mauss, Marcel, *The Gift, Forms and Function of Exchange in Archaic Societies*, trans. I. Cunnison, Cohen & West, 1954.

NOTES. — 1. This article concerns the Negro revue "Lew Leslie's Black Birds," at the Moulin Rouge, June-September 1929. [Author's note.]

2. In ch. 26 of *Exploits and Opinions of Doctor Faustroll, 'Pataphysician*.

3. This extraordinary film is the work of two young Catalans: the painter Salvador Dali, and the director Luis Buñuel. See the excellent stills published by *Cahiers d'Art* (July 1929, p. 230), by *Bifur* (August 1929, p. 105) and by *Variétés* (July 1929, p. 209). This film can be distinguished from the banal productions of the avant-garde, with which one might be tempted to confuse it, by the importance given to the screenplay. Several very explicit facts follow one upon the other, without logical connection it is true, but penetrating so deeply into horror that the spectators are caught up as directly as they are in an adventure film. More precisely, they are caught by the throat, and without artifice: do they know, in fact, how far the authors of this film, or people like them, will go? If Buñuel himself, after filming the slitting open of the eye, was ill for a week (and he then had to film the scene of the asses' cadavers in a pestilential atmosphere), how can one not appreciate the extent of horror's fascination, and that it alone is sufficient to shatter everything that stifles us? [Author's note.]

4. Victor Hugo, a reader of *Le Magazin pittoresque*, borrowed from both the admirable dream narrative *Crime and Expiation,* and from the unprecedented drawing of Grandville, both published in 1847 (pp. 211-14), the story of the pursuit of a criminal by an obstinate eye: it is scarcely useful to observe, however, that only an obscure and sinister obsession, and not a cold memory, can explain this resemblance. We owe to Pierre d'Espezel's erudition and generosity our awareness of this curious document, probably the most beautiful of Grandville's extravagant compositions. [Author's note.]

5. *Faire suer un chêne* has this literal meaning, but is also argot for killing someone (i.e. the oak fears being made into a coffin).

6. Bucrane or Bucranium: an architectural ornament taking the form of an ox-skull.

7. The followers of Pythagoras were forbidden (among other things) to eat beans. Islam enjoins ablution before prayer; in the absence of water, sand may be used.

8. American journalist (1868-1940). The book was first published in Britain in 1927 as *Mother India*. Its sensationalism provoked the indignation of Indian nationalists and British anti-imperialists.

9. The English original, *The Blood-Guiltiness of Christendom (May We Slay For Food?)*, was published in 1922 by The Order of the Golden Age, which seems to have been a group of militant nationalist vegetarians. Other works include: *The Murder of Agriculture, Socialism and its Perils, Britain for the Briton* and *Spiritual Science, Here and Hereafter*. The quotation is from page 33.

10. Pensum, according to the OED: "A charge, duty, or allotted task; a school-task or lesson to be prepared; also (U.S.) a lesson or piece of work imposed as a punishment, a school 'imposition.' "

11. The Platonic, Great, or Perfect year (Annus Magnus), was estimated by early Greek astronomers at about 26,000 years, at the end of which all the heavenly bodies are imagined to have returned to the places they occupied at the creation.

12. Laius was Oedipus's father. Phaeton, the son of Helios (the sun-god), sought to drive his father's chariot, came a cropper and thereby turned Libya into a parched desert and blackened the inhabitants of Africa; Zeus saved the world from being destroyed by fire by shooting him down.

13. In *The Magic Island*. [Author's note.]

14. Henri Bergson (1859-1941). Philosopher, the titles of whose main works, *Creative Evolution*, and *Matter and Memory*, give some idea of the general idealist direction of his thought.

15. Emile Meyerson (1859-1933). Philosopher of science, opposed to the positivist and empiricist views of many of his colleagues, holding that hypothesis is necessarily prior to research.

16. Eugène Minkowski (1885-1972). Psychiatrist: his work on schizophrenia and *"le temps vécu,"* lived time, (the inspiration for which derives from Bergson) follows in the philosophical tradition of French psychiatry.

17. Hanoteaux & Letourneux, *Kabylie*, III, p. 193. [Author's note.]

18. *Koran*, Sura 113. [Author's note.]

19. Marcel Griaule, *Le Livre de recettes d'un dabtara abyssin*, Institut d'ethnologie de Paris. [Author's note.]

20. Marcelle Vessereau, *"L'Adret et l'Ubac dans les Alpes occidentales."* Annales de Géographie, 15 Sept. 1921 (XXXe Année, no. 167), pp. 321-3. For the same phenomenon in the Swiss Alps: Ch. Biermann, *Le Val de Conches-en-Valais. Essai sur la vie dans une haute vallée des Alpes suisses sous l'influence de l'altitude, du climat et du relief*, Lausanne, 1907, 8vo. [Author's note.]

21. J. Ch. F. Baron de Ladoucette: *Histoire, antiquités, usages des Hautes-Alpes, précédés d'un essai sur la topographie de ce département*, Paris, Fantin, 1820, 8vo., CLX, 208pp. [Author's note.]

22. See an essay on the relationship between festivals and the seasonal life of Eskimos: Hubert & Mauss, *Année Sociologique*, old series. Their results are applied in a study of the popular festival that preceded Christmas, *Arch. de Religion suisse*, 1916. [Author's note.]

23. Apropos of *Weary River*, showing at the Clichy-Palace cinema, September 1929. [Author's note.]

24. *Bulletin de l'Art ancien et moderne*, Sept.-Oct. 1929, p. 338. [Author's note.] Dongen (1877-1968) was a painter, originally associated with the anarchistic satirical review *L'Assiette au Beurre* around the turn of the century. Later an associate of Picasso, he then became a somewhat celebrated "society" portrait painter.

25. In *L'Anthropologie*, 1903, pp. 733-6; reprinted in *Cultes, mythes et religions*, 1905, vol. I, pp. 105-10. [Author's note.]

26. By 1921, when Tristan Tzara acknowledged that the absence of system is still a system, but of the most sympathetic sort, "this concession to insignificant objections still apparently remained inconsequential; the introduction of Hegelianism soon to follow, however, could then be expected. The step from this admission to Hegel's panlogism is an easy one, since it is consistent with the principle of the identity of contradictory terms. We may even suppose that once this treachery was committed, there was no way of avoiding this panlogism and its glaring consequences, by which I mean the sordid thirst for completeness in all things, a blind hypocrisy, and, ultimately, the need to serve anything that is determinate. Despite the fact that these vulgar inclinations have, in compromise with a diametrically opposed impulse, most felicitously exacerbated certain agreed-upon difficulties, there is, from this point on, no further reason not to reconsider the futile betrayal expressed by Tristan Tzara. It is impossible, really, to see what can be systematic in the savage opposition to all system, unless a pun is involved, and the word systematic is understood in the common sense of mechanical obstination. But this is no matter for joking, and this pun betrays, for once, a fundamental, wretched senility. There is really no difference between humility, of the slightest degree, before the SYSTEM — which is to say, before the Idea — and the fear of God. Moreover, this lamentable statement seems — and with reason — literally to have throttled Tzara, who has since displayed a complete sluggishness. This statement appeared as an epigraph in a book by Louis Aragon (*Anicet*, Paris,

1921). [Author's note.]

27. Another reading of *La Da Costa Encyclopèdique* would be "The Complete Da Costa."

28. *Echecs* means "chess," while *echec* means "check" in chess, and also "failure."

29. Allusion to Louis XIV's *"L'état c'est moi,"* "I am the state." We have been unable to discover what the poster question advertised.

30. *Le Parc aux Cerfs* (at Versailles): described in the *Oxford Companion to French Literature* as "the notorious seraglio of Louis XV." So called because built on the site of a former deer-park.

31. See Mario Praz, *The Romantic Agony,* ch. 3, n. 58: "the Bleeding Nun was the ghost of a woman who was forced by her parents to become a nun, but who did not resist the impulses of her 'warm and voluptuous character' and abandoned herself to all sorts of excesses, committed murder, and was herself murdered." The same work casts light on *Thérèse Philosophe* mentioned a few lines earlier, which Praz describes as a "coarse piece of pornographic fiction" by Darles de Montigny (1748). The story of The Bleeding Nun was incorporated into Chapter Four of Matthew Lewis' gothic novel *The Monk* (1796).

32. This myth being one of those featured in the exhibition *First Papers of Surrealism*, held in New York in 1942.

33. Who has already appeared in *The Critical Dictionary* (**Bonjour Brothers**).

34. Mark 9. 12.

35. On 2 September 1792, twenty-five priests (16 in other accounts), suspected of involvement in royalist plots and collusion with the invading Prussians, were subjected to summary execution by an enraged crowd in the course of their being transferred from the Hôtel de Ville and the Abbaye prison. On this occasion the Abbé Picard, head of the Deaf-and-Dumb Institute, and his assistant, were spared.

36. This text, undoubtedly by the Roussel scholar Jean Ferry, alludes to chapter six of Roussel's novel *Locus Solus.*

37. An emmenagogue is, in fact, a medicine intended to stimulate menstruation; thus often a euphemism for an abortifacient. As to the critic pilloried here, the reference remains obscure.

38. Abel Hermant (1862-1950). Novelist, essayist and critic. His *Grammaire de l'Académie Française* (1932) provoked hostile criticism and fell quickly into oblivion.

39. Polygon presumably meaning *hexagone,* a common expression for France.

40. An encomiast is an utterer of fulsome praises. A paranymph, in English, is a groomsman or bridesmaid; here, the sense is a friend of a candidate for the licentiate in medicine or theology who, in ancient times, accompanied him to the examination and solemnly complimented him on his admission.

41. Barthélemy-Prosper Enfantin (1796-1864). French "utopian" socialist, and the leader of the followers of Saint-Simon after the latter's death. A charismatic character, the movement grew rapidly under his direction and was eventually suppressed when Enfantin was convicted of outraging public morals. His crime: extending the Saint-Simonian demand for the total emancipation of women to that of the destruction of "the tyranny of marriage," and preaching the androgynous nature of the deity. The movement declined after this and his journey to Egypt; he spent his later years in various low-paid positions in the the state bureaucracy, still convinced of the accuracy of his convictions. Enfantin also makes an appearance in Breton's *Arcane 17.*

42. One legend has it that Lady Hester Stanhope, the explorer and Arabist, was approached, but declined the role.

43. René Etiemble, critic and essayist. His *Le Mythe de Rimbaud* attempted to demystify the poet, in the process criticising the Surrealists. For this and other actions he earned their continued hostility, which, it must be said, was shared by many other literary figures.

44. *Freddo*: "coldness" in Italian.

45. Stendhal's real name was Beyle.

46. Jacques Delille (1738-1813). Poet, his insipid works had a brief popularity.

47. The star-crossed lovers in *The Charterhouse of Parma*.

48. *Aventures de Télémaque*. A "didactic romance" by Fénélon (1699), one of the classics of French literature.

49. These events actually occurred. Olivier Laronde, born 1927, died in 1965, insisted on the corrections being made, and Sartre complied, perhaps rather unwillingly.

50. Allusion to the notice: "It is forbidden to deposit rubbish on the public highway."

51. From the sixth *Document to Serve as an Outline* by Raymond Roussel (pp. 56-64 of the Atlas Press edition of *Selections from Certain of His Books*).

52. Apparently [cf. F2, 229] this article so outraged Robert and her family that they spent several months verbally abusing various suspected authors, but failed to identify the one actually responsible.

53. Administrative jargon for citizens of French overseas territories, e.g. Algeria, French West Africa, Martinique etc.

54. Joseph de Maistre (1753-1821). Catholic philosopher. A monarchist, he held that the king's sovereignty was absolute, subject only to his supporting the pope's authority. A supporter of papal infallibility.

55. In French *ces pustuleux du bénitier*, an extra richness is added to the phrase by the fact that *bénitier* not only means holy-water-font but is one of the many slang expressions for the female genitals.

56. See the same author's *Sade mon prochain*. [Author's note.] Ferry's scorn of Klossowski, an old member of Acéphale, is based on his retaining his Catholic faith, despite professing an admiration for Sade etc.

57. In the French *faire leurs besoins religieux* also refers to the polite expression *faire ses besoins*, attend to a call of nature.

58. Gaston de Gallifet (1830-1909). French general infamous for his bloody suppression of the Paris Commune of 1871.

59. To be found on pp. 16 and 21 of *The Annotated Snark* (Penguin) edited by Martin Gardner, among other places.

60. In the picture, painted in 1927, a pair of figures dressed in doublet and hose, but headless, thrash about in an empty room while another, rather similar figure enters menacingly by the window. This is presumably an oblique reference to the 1946 denunciation by Andrei Zhdanov, Secretary of the Central Committtee of the CPSU of the "decadence" and "formalism" of Soviet writers (he named Akhmatova and Zoschenko), in which he singled out members of the Leningrad Writer's Union. Breton and the Surrealists were the only left-aligned intellectuals (with the exception of Souvarine's group) to attack these abuses at this time.

61. 6.023 x 10^{23}. Duchamp's *griffe volante* remains obscure: Breton praises his picture *Coeurs volantes* in *Arcane 17*, and perhaps this is what is meant here (there are a number of typos in the *Da Costa*).

62. "The Star" is Arcanum 17 of the Tarot pack, the principal linking theme of Breton's *Arcane 17* written around this time.

63. This article presumably concerns "Gödel's Proof." Put briefly, around the turn of the century the mathematician David Hilbert attempted to make the foundations of mathematics consistent by establishing them on an axiomatic basis similar to geometry and then formalising the whole deductive system by "draining" mathematical signs of meaning and describing them in a mathematical meta-language. All went swimmingly until an unknown mathematician, Kurt Gödel, proved that if mathematics was consistent, it would not be able to demonstrate that consistency either mathematically or meta-mathematically. In other words, certain fundamentals of mathematics remain unprovable within the system of mathematics itself.

64. Eponymous hero of the novella by Heinrich Kleist (1810).

65. Possibly a reference to Verlaine's epithet for Rimbaud: *l'homme aux semelles de vent* (the man shod with the wind).

66. A system first proposed by Alphonse Allais in his story *The Smell-Buoy*, in *Amours, délices et orgues* (1898).

67. To French readers, especially at the time this was written, the word *exode*, exodus, would evoke not so much the Bible, more the flight in 1940 of countless civilians before the Nazi invaders.

68. The word is not in standard French dictionaries. The OED defines it as meaning gone out of use, obsolete, effete, insipid; Clazomenae according to Lemprière's Classical Dictionary was a city on the Aegean coast, between Smyrna and Chios, birthplace of the philosopher Anaxagoras.

69. The 1863-72 *Littré Dictionnaire* classes the word as *med.*, and derives it from the Greek εξ (out of) and ονειρος (a dream); definition: *pollution nocturne*, nocturnal pollution, i.e. a wet dream. The word has vanished from 20th century dictionaries.

70. Cornelius Sulla, died 78 BC, Roman dictator, who retired from power and restored constitutional government in order to devote his last years to his memoirs, a 24 book apologia for his past excesses: they have not survived.

71. The article exploits this double-meaning of the French *Exposition*.

72. As the final sentence makes plain, this text is an attack on the sound poetry of Isidore Isou's Lettrist movement founded in 1946 around the review *La Dictature lettriste* and Isou's manifesto *Pour une nouvelle poésie, pour une nouvelle musique* (Gallimard). The birds' songs do indeed bear a strong resemblance to the bizarre poems in this book in which Isou's megalomania was first committed to print.

Les Amis de Georges Bataille may be contacted via
Dominique Lecoq
16, rue de l'Echiquier
75010 Paris.

ARKHIVE I: DADA BERLIN

THE DADA ALMANAC. *Edited by Richard Huelsenbeck, Berlin, 1920. Introduced and annotated by Malcolm Green & Alastair Brotchie. Translated by Malcolm Green, Barbara Wright & Derk Wynand. Illustrations, biographies, etc. 176 pp. £12.99/$19.99. (In print.)*

THE DADA ALMANAC was assembled by Richard Huelsenbeck, one of the foremost Dadaists from the very inception of Dada to its end, and published in Berlin in 1920 at the high-point of Dadaist activities in the German capital: the *Dada Almanac* was and is the most important single Dadaist publication. Containing a wide range of poetry, polemics, essays, manifestos and deliberate confusions, not only does it present the vast range of Dadaist literary production and experimentation on an international scale, it also reveals many of the apparent contradictions which lie at the heart of the movement. Extra editorial matter, texts, and photographs have been added to this edition.

This annotated version of the Almanac, *the first to appear in English, is a crucial document for anyone interested in the history of the 20th century avant-garde.* —The New York Times Book Review. The Dada Almanac *is an excellent place to experience Dadaism in its own terms and in all its contradictions ... If there's a reason that the Dadaists appeal to our own cultural confusions, it can undoubtedly be discovered here.* —Los Angeles Times. *...still thrilling, still weird.* —Artforum.

ARKHIVE II: FRENCH SYMBOLIST & DECADENT WRITING OF THE 1890S

THE BOOK OF MASKS. *Essays by Remy de Gourmont, with authors' texts selected by Andrew Mangravite. Translated by Andrew Mangravite, Iain White, Terry Hale & others. Illustrations, biographies, 304 pp. £13.99/$19.99. (In print.)*

THE BOOK OF MASKS was published in two parts in 1896 and 1898 and consists of essays on the most important of his Symbolist contemporaries by the foremost critic and author of the period: Remy de Gourmont. (The "masks" referred to in the title are the series of remarkable portraits of the authors drawn by Felix Vallotton.) Each author is represented in this edition by texts from the period; de Gourmont's prefaces to each volume, and overviews of the Symbolists and their preoccupations are included. The works of forty-seven authors are featured, many never before translated into English.

Symbolism was a strange amalgam of the social turmoil of the time; its authors veered between an aesthetics based on simplicity and asceticism and the decadent debauches forever associated with Huysmans and Wilde. Their political associations were equally split, between Catholic piety and right-wing nationalism (Claudel, Barrès) and the anarchist individualism of Tailhade and Fénéon. What united these disparate writers at their best was a fierce literature based on a renewed use of language, finely tuned, often astonishingly lush, and aimed at an intense examination of the borderland between inner and outer life.

A chrestomathy of enchantments for readers whose capacity for wonder is rarely exercised by what passes for literature today. —The Spectator. *A rich cache of relatively unknown writers . . . just the thing to give a neurasthenic idler for Christmas.* —The Guardian.

ARKHIVE IV (AUTUMN 1995): FLUXUS

AN ANECDOTED TOPOGRAPHY OF CHANCE. *Daniel Spoerri, in collaboration with Robert Filliou, Emmett Williams and Dieter Rot, illustrations by Topor. 180 pp. approx. £13.99/$19.99.*

FLUXUS was a loose association of American and European artists operating throughout the sixties and seventies, and the present book is the result of a long-term collaboration between four of its most perceptive and good-humoured participants. It not only personifies the whole Fluxus spirit, but also constitutes a semi-autobiography of an important section of the movement. What is the Topography? Hard to explain the resonance of such a simple idea so brilliantly executed: Spoerri maps the objects left at random on his table one day (the map appears inside the original edition's dustwrapper). He writes about them, their associations; his friends write about what he writes, anecdotes, recipes, recollections, asides, footnotes upon footnotes proliferate: it is life itself in all its chaos as revealed by four sharp, witty and congenial members of the human species.

The Atlas Press edition will be a reformatted version of the famous *Something Else Press* edition of 1966, to which we will add, for the first time in English, the annotations of Dieter Rot, who anecdoted the German edition while translating it. There will be a new introduction by Spoerri, Wllliams, Rot & Topor, extra photographs and texts.

   ● *A numbered edition, in a different cover and slipcase, limited to 100 copies and signed by Spoerri, Williams, Rot & Topor will be available.*

ARKHIVE V (SUMMER 1996): THE OULIPO & ITS OFFSPRING

AN OULIPO COMPENDIUM. *Edited in collaboration with Harry Mathews & Thieri Foulc. Translations by Harry Mathews & others. Illustrations, maps, games, biographies, manifestos etc. 176 pp.*

The **OULIPO** was founded in 1960 by the author Raymond Queneau and the mathematician/chess-player François LeLionnais, originally to investigate the possibilities of combining mathematics and literature. Oulipo stands for *Ouvroir de littérature potentielle* (roughly "Workshop of Potential Literature"). The group's preoccupations soon widened to include all aspects of "constrictive form" in writing, from simple forms like the sonnet to an entire novel written with words lacking the letter "e" (Perec's *La Disparition*). The group has met monthly for 30 years now and publishes its own *Bibliothèque Oulipienne* (more than 70 publications) as well as anthologies of their collective activities. This compendium will also include examples of Oulipian methods used by various American authors (Gilbert Sorrentino, Dallas Wiebe, Keith Waldrop, etc.). The Oulipo has spawned numerous versions of itself devoted to constrictive form in other areas: the Oulipopo (*Ouvroir de littérature potentielle policier* = "Workshop for potential detective fiction"); the Oupeinpo applies similar methods to painting.

Authors (Oulipo) include: *Noël Arnaud, Marcel Bénabou, Claude Bens, Italo Calvino, François Caradec, Stanley Chapman, Marcel Duchamp, Luc Étienne, Paul Fournel, Jacques Jouet, Latis, François LeLionnais, Jean Lescure, Harry Mathews, Michèle Métail, Oskar Pastior, Georges Perec, Raymond Queneau, Jacques Roubaud.* Artists (Oupeinpo): *Jacques Carelman, Jean Dewasne, Thieri Foulc, Aline Gagnaire.*

   ● *A numbered edition, in a different cover and slipcase, limited to 100 copies and signed by all current members of both groups will be available.*